···☽ THE ZENNED OUT GUIDE TO ☾···

UNDERSTANDING

CRYSTALS

First published in 2020 by Rock Point,
an imprint of The Quarto Group
142 West 36th Street, 4th Floor
New York, NY 10018, USA
T (212) 779-4972 F (212) 779-6058
www.QuartoKnows.com

Rock Point titles are also available at discount for retail, wholesale, promotional, and bulk purchase. For details, contact the Special Sales Manager by email at specialsales@quarto.com or by mail at The Quarto Group, Attn: Special Sales Manager, 100 Cummings Center Suite 265D, Beverly, MA 01915 USA.

10 9 8 7 6

ISBN: 978-1-63106-707-5

Library of Congress Cataloging-in-Publication Data

Names: Uhl, Cassie, author.
Title: The Zenned Out guide to understanding crystals : your handbook to using and connecting to crystal energy / Cassie Uhl.
Other titles: Understanding crystals : your handbook to using and connecting to crystal energy
Description: New York : Rock Point, 2020. | Series: Zenned Out | Summary: "The Zenned Out Guide to Understanding Crystals is an introduction to the mystical energy of crystals. Part of the Zenned Out series, this book includes easy-to-digest actionable steps to enable readers to get started right away"-- Provided by publisher.
Identifiers: LCCN 2020007151 (print) | LCCN 2020007152 (ebook) | ISBN 9781631067075 (hardcover) | ISBN 9780760367858 (ebook)
Subjects: LCSH: Crystals--Psychic aspects. | Crystals--Miscellanea.
Classification: LCC BF1442.C78 U35 2020 (print) | LCC BF1442.C78 (ebook) | DDC 133/.2548--dc23
LC record available at https://lccn.loc.gov/2020007151
LC ebook record available at https://lccn.loc.gov/2020007152

PUBLISHER: Rage Kindelsperger
CREATIVE DIRECTOR: Laura Drew
MANAGING EDITOR: Cara Donaldson
EDITOR: Keyla Pizarro-Hernández
COVER AND INTERIOR DESIGN: Sydney Martenis

Printed in China

THE ZENNED OUT GUIDE TO

UNDERSTANDING
CRYSTALS

YOUR HANDBOOK TO USING AND
CONNECTING TO CRYSTAL ENERGY

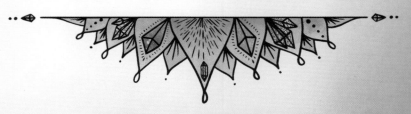

CASSIE UHL

ROCK
POINT

The recent fascination with crystals signals a shift in the human collective. People are seemingly drawn in by the healing powers of them. I believe our energy as a collective is becoming more aligned with crystals. Whether you're brand new to working with crystals or have been captivated by them for years, this book will deepen your crystal wisdom. You'll find guidance and tools throughout to understand and work with the energy of crystals in new and enlightening ways.

My viewpoint on crystals is one of energy. This book, your body, and crystals are composed of energy that vibrates at different frequencies. Energy is fluid and impressionable. If your energy is vibrating at the same frequency as a crystal, it explains why you may feel drawn to that crystal.

Though we're all energy, crystals have an exceptional composition. They are comprised of perfectly repeated atoms. The flawless arrangement of energy within crystals is their superpower. They radiate their perfection outward, and anything within their range will benefit.

AT THE SMALLEST LEVEL, EVERYTHING IS ENERGY.

Crystals can affect our energy in a variety of ways, and even the most skeptical of people can find ways to work with them.

Beyond their ability to heal, crystals also offer us a unique intention-setting tool. When using crystals in this way, you're relying on the power of your mind to initiate change; the crystal serves as a reminder of the change you want to create. Every crystal has a unique meaning associated with it based on its color, structure, and individual energy frequency. The healing properties associated with each one can serve as a reminder to act in a way that's in alignment with your desires.

REASONS TO WORK WITH CRYSTALS

- To remind you of the energy you're trying to bring into your life

- To manifest specific items and goals

- To heal your subtle energy system

- To identify your soul path

- To protect and cleanse your energy or the energy of your environment

- To use in ritual and magick work

In this book, I share a variety of ways to work with crystal energy. You'll learn techniques for everyday uses, such as being calmer throughout your day as well as methods for using crystals to connect with your spirit, so you better understand your purpose.

I'm a firm believer in the power of unseen energies around us. I've been meditating and working with the energy of my chakras from a young age. I've always been drawn to crystals and have relied on them as an intention-setting tool for years. As an adult, when I began to learn more about their innate healing abilities, I wasn't surprised. Learning this about crystals connected the dots, and all of my knowledge about energy made more sense.

I have a beautiful clear quartz crystal that I've had in my possession for a long time. I believe that this little quartz has been imparting its healing energy to me throughout every phase of my life, even before I fully understood crystal energy. Today, it lives in my shop and studio and serves as a constant reminder of the power of crystals.

Now, I work with a variety of crystals daily as the owner of my own company, Zenned Out. They are a part of my energy work in my spiritual practice. Every day, I make a conscious decision about what kind of energy I want to bring into my meditation, my work, and my aura. I do this by selecting specific stones to work with during meditation, wearing crystals that bring in the energy I feel I need, and placing specific stones near me as I work. I know that every crystal brings me unique energy. If I am in a state of conscious awareness, I will feel that energy, and it will affect everything I do.

CRYSTAL ETHICS

If you're interested in working with crystals, it's necessary to discuss crystal ethics before we begin. Anytime a physical commodity increases in popularity, it's essential that we're aware of the processes involved with taking crystals from the earth and selling them. Even though crystals seem so innately peaceful, many have made a very long journey from the earth to your hands.

The spiritual connotation of crystals leads many to believe that they must be mined, cut, and delivered to each retailer in the most ethical way possible. Unfortunately, this is far from the truth. Many crystals are mined in unsafe environments, by workers who are rarely compensated with fair wages.

From an environmental impact perspective, the life of a single crystal may travel great distances between being mined, cut, and sold. The incredible distances our crystals travel creates a large carbon footprint. Though you may not be able to find all of your favorite crystals locally, I suggest being mindful about how often you're purchasing crystals from other countries. These issues may seem insurmountable, but change begins with you. As consumers, we need to demand ethically sourced crystals. Doing so will force suppliers to follow suit.

If you already have a collection of crystals and aren't sure whether they were mined and made ethically, don't let it prevent you from working with them. You don't know what you know until you know it. Many books on the topic of crystals neglect to inform its readers of crystal ethics. Go ahead and release any guilt you may have about how your current crystals came to you and opt for ethically sourced crystals moving forward. Check out the list below for suggestions on acquiring ethically sourced crystals.

◄◡ HOW TO PURCHASE ETHICAL CRYSTALS ◡►

♦ Mine your own crystals.

♦ Purchase directly from crystal miners.

♦ Purchase from crystal sellers who are transparent and ethical about where they purchase their crystals.

♦ Ask crystal sellers whether their crystals are mined and formed ethically and only purchase if they can provide you with an acceptable answer.

·◦D TIP ◁◦·

Purchasing ethically may limit your options but will bring you crystals that carry the purest energy. Think quality over quantity.

CRYSTALS THROUGHOUT HISTORY

Looking at the artwork of many ancient cultures leaves little doubt about the use of crystals in history. Ancient Egyptians relied heavily on turquoise and lapis lazuli as adornments, protective talismans, and cure-alls. Ancient Sumerians mention the use of crystals in magick formulas, and Chinese medicine relies on the healing power of crystals as well.

···◈ HOW TO USE THIS BOOK ◈···

I created this book to offer you a potent reference guide for experiencing crystal energy. It can be read from beginning to end for a deep understanding of how crystals impart their energy to us, what their healing properties are, and how to work with their energy. This book can also be used as a quick reference guide for crystal properties. If a specific chapter calls to you, trust your instincts, and go to it first. My singular request is that you approach each chapter with an open mind!

PAUSE.
ASK FOR
DIRECTION.
WAIT FOR
GUIDANCE.

CHAPTER 1

HOW CRYSTAL ENERGY WORKS

There are a variety of ways that crystal energy can affect your mind, body, and subtle energy systems. Let's break down some of the mystery behind why and how crystals work, so you can better understand them and feel confident about their healing abilities.

Beyond the scientific structure of crystals, there are some fascinating metaphysical perspectives on crystal energy. Now, I'm going to say something that might shock you. You can use crystals as a healing tool, even if you don't believe that crystal energy is real. There are so many ways to benefit from crystal energy that you don't need to believe they can work for them to work!

There are a variety of ways that crystals can cause a change in your subtle or physical body, for believers and nonbelievers alike. My first explanation of how crystal energy works is my go-to for skeptics and anyone new to them.

CRYSTALS AS AN INTENTION-SETTING TOOL

I've always been inquisitive, and even though I've been into all things metaphysical and spiritual from a young age, I didn't immediately jump on the crystal wagon. The idea of using crystals as an intention-setting tool is exactly where I started when I began my crystal journey years ago.

·◦◊ TIP ◊◦·

Working with crystals as an intention-setting tool is the best place for any skeptic or beginner.

What I mean by using a crystal as an intention-setting tool is that you keep a crystal nearby as a reminder of your goals and desires. That's it. No fluff, no woo-woo. If you are seeking more love in your life, you can work with rose quartz simply as a reminder that you're open to accepting more love in your life. If you carry a piece of rose quartz around in your pocket with the intention of allowing love into your life, you will remember that intention every time you feel the stone in your pocket. Working with crystals can be nothing more than this, and it is still powerful.

YOUR ENERGY FLOWS WHERE YOUR INTENTION GOES.

Do I believe that crystals have more to offer? Yes, but you don't have to. Even when we get into more detailed crystal work with crystal grids and crystal rituals later in the book, this same intention-setting idea can be applied. Setting up a crystal grid requires you to focus intently on your desires, and this in and of itself is a powerful manifesting tool! If you're on the fence about the legitimacy of crystal healing but feel drawn to them, this is all you need to know. I encourage you to continue working with them and see how your life begins to shift and change as you do.

CRYSTALS AND
TRACE ELEMENTS

At a physical level, every crystal contains a unique makeup of trace elements. Your skin can absorb the trace elements within crystals, which can affect your physical body. For example, turquoise and malachite both contain copper. Copper is an essential nutrient for our bodies and can be beneficial when used appropriately. Our ancestors understood this about specific stones, and it's one reason why turquoise and malachite were both prized by ancient Egyptians.

Many crystals are toxic if consumed, so this method of working with crystals isn't recommended unless you have an in-depth understanding of the body and trace elements. I discuss this in more detail on page 53, when I cover gem elixirs.

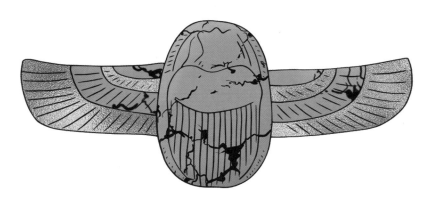

EGYPTIAN AMULET

CRYSTALS AND THE PLACEBO EFFECT

Now, will crystals work better for you if you do believe that they can affect your energy? Yes, absolutely! If you're not there yet, that's okay. Think of crystals as another tool in your magickal tool belt. I do hope that you are 100 percent convinced about the power of crystals by the time you finish this book.

If we put on our scientist lenses, we can look at crystal energy from the perspective of the placebo effect. The placebo effect has been thoroughly documented. If you believe wholeheartedly that crystal energy is real, it will have an effect on you. What you believe to be true will influence your subtle energy body and your physical body. If you think something will bring you more love, you'll act in a way that will open you up to more love.

YOUR THOUGHTS ARE POWERFUL.

CRYSTALS ARE
PERFECT STRUCTURES

Now let's look at some of the science of crystals and how crystal healers believe they can change and shift our energy.

When crystals form, their atoms create a perfect repeating lattice. This crystalline lattice will repeat as the crystal takes shape. If the pattern is a square, for example, the result will be a cube-shaped crystal, such as pyrite. All authentic crystals form in this way, with a cohesive repeating lattice structure.

There are seven crystal systems, or crystal formations: triclinic, monoclinic, orthorhombic, tetragonal, trigonal, hexagonal, and cubic. Beyond this, crystals break down into even more classifications. The scientific study of crystals and how they form is called crystallography. If you are intrigued by the study of crystal formations, I encourage you to research it further.

Because of the perfectly repeated structures within crystals, their energy is not easily disturbed. They have an extremely stable makeup at the atomic level, which makes the energy that they radiate outward stable as well. This innate perfection within crystals is also why they are great at storing information. Many in the metaphysical community, myself included, believe it is the perfect structure within crystals that enables them to retain information and radiate it outward so powerfully.

···✦ CRYSTAL SYSTEMS ✦···

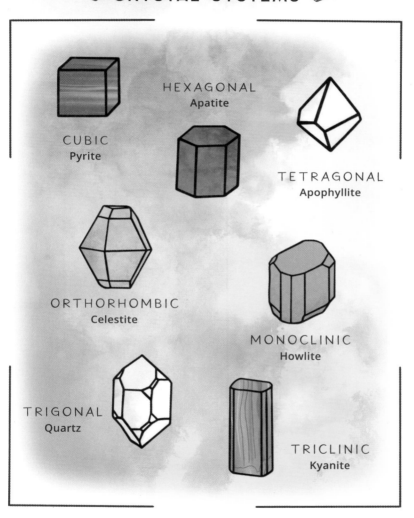

CUBIC
Pyrite

HEXAGONAL
Apatite

TETRAGONAL
Apophyllite

ORTHORHOMBIC
Celestite

MONOCLINIC
Howlite

TRIGONAL
Quartz

TRICLINIC
Kyanite

The ways that crystals form naturally or are cut and polished will affect how they radiate their energy outward. Pointed crystals direct their energy out of the points. The directional flow of pointed crystals is why geode-type crystals, with many small points, make potent crystal chargers and cleansers. The flow of energy from pointed crystals is why healers like to work with this shape. The energy healer can direct the energy of the crystal to a specific point on the body.

Alternatively, a sphere will radiate its energy out equally in all directions. For this reason, spheres are lovely to have in the home, because they create a gentle blanket of crystal energy. I dive deeper into crystal shapes, the way they radiate their energy, and suggested uses in chapter 6.

Some stones are called "crystals," but they are not true crystals. For example, stones that cool very quickly don't have time to form a crystalline structure. Stones in this category aren't actual crystals because they don't contain a crystalline structure. One example is amber, which is fossilized tree resin. However, you can still work with gemstones that aren't actual crystals and benefit from their healing energy, though you may find that it's less potent.

GEMSTONES WITHOUT CRYSTALLINE STRUCTURES

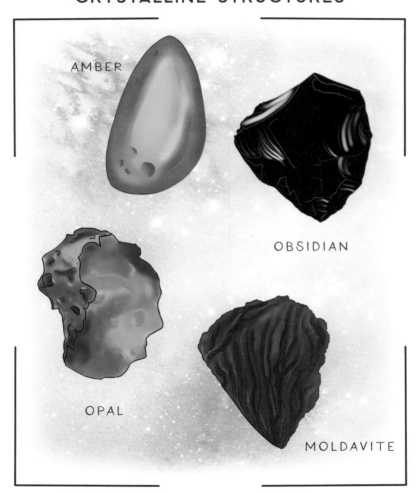

AMBER

OBSIDIAN

OPAL

MOLDAVITE

ENTRAINMENT AND THE
LAW OF ATTRACTION

As I've already mentioned and will continue to say, everything is energy. Every person and object, at the smallest level, has a vibrational frequency. *Entrainment* explains what happens when one vibrating frequency matches that of another. When two different vibrating frequencies occupy the same space, they cannot remain in the same space at the same time. They entrain, or synchronize, with one another at the same vibrational frequency.

You can demonstrate entrainment with two tuning forks. If you strike a tuning fork, it emits a vibrational frequency. If you hit another tuning fork and bring it near the first, the first one will take on the same vibrational frequency as the second one. You can watch videos of this being performed online or try it out for yourself!

SURROUND YOURSELF WITH THE KIND OF
ENERGY YOU WANT TO ATTRACT.

The law of attraction is based on the idea of entrainment. Two completely different frequencies cannot exist in the same time and space. For example, if you are continually telling yourself that you're broke, you will vibrate at a frequency of lack. The energy frequency of being broke can't live with the energy frequency of abundance. To be abundant, you'll need to shift your energy frequency to entrain, or be in alignment, with the frequency of abundance.

This same principle of entrainment can be applied to working with crystals. Because crystals emit such a cohesive and structured frequency, a crystal forces whatever is around it to entrain with its frequency. For example, if you're working with a high-vibrational stone, like selenite, your energy frequency will try to match its vibration. As you explore the different healing properties of crystals in chapter 2, you'll be able to better understand what kind of energy each crystal emits.

Entrainment explains why you'll feel deeply pulled to some crystals and repelled by others. If the vibrational frequency of a crystal is very different from yours, you may feel uncomfortable when you're around the crystal. The reason for your discomfort is because two incompatible vibrational frequencies—your energy and that of the crystal—are trying to occupy the same space. If your energy is unable to merge with that of the crystal's, the crystal will repel you.

The famous psychic, Edgar Cayce (1877–1945), wrote extensively about the vibratory frequencies of crystals, how their colors affect us, and the power of programming them. Cayce was especially fond of lapis lazuli and promoted it as a stone of "spiritual energy" and "attunement." Many metaphysical topics are based on entrainment. If you feel compelled to explore this topic more, you may find work regarding the law of attraction interesting.

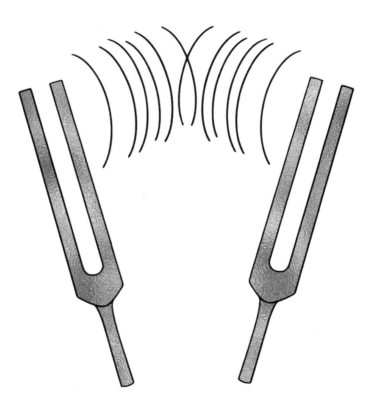

CRYSTALS AND ELECTRICITY

Did you know that quartz crystals are used in a variety of technologies, helping our modern age thrive in multiple ways? Quartz, along with topaz and tourmaline, can create an electric current when it is heated (pyroelectricity), or when pressure or sound waves are applied to it (piezoelectricity). Even pressing a quartz-based crystal in your hands will create an electric current. This is why quartz is used in ultrasound technology, radios, computers, TVs, watches, and other applications.

Marcel Vogel (1917–1991) worked specifically with quartz crystal and conducted scientific experiments with it while working for IBM. He later formulated a unique quartz crystal cut intended to be used for healing. It was given the name "Vogel crystal" and can direct and amplify energy. There are only a few people in the world trained to cut authentic Vogel crystals, and these crystals come at a high price.

As the scientific community continues to deepen its understanding of quantum physics, it seems that more and more wisdom from our ancestors and modern "mystical" beliefs are true. If some of this seems too far-fetched for you, I invite you to perform your own experiments in working with crystals. You can wait for science to catch up with what many healers and mystics already know to be true, or you can begin enjoying the healing benefits of crystals now. It's hard to imagine that the idea of germs used to be fanciful thinking! Just because science can't fully explain how crystals work doesn't mean that they don't affect us.

PYROELECTRIC AND PIEZOELECTRIC CRYSTALS

- ◆ Quartz family
  - ✦ Agate
  - ✦ Amethyst
  - ✦ Aventurine
  - ✦ Carnelian
  - ✦ Citrine
  - ✦ Jasper
- ✦ Onyx
- ✦ Rose quartz
- ✦ Smoky quartz
- ✦ Tiger eye
- ◆ Topaz
- ◆ Tourmaline

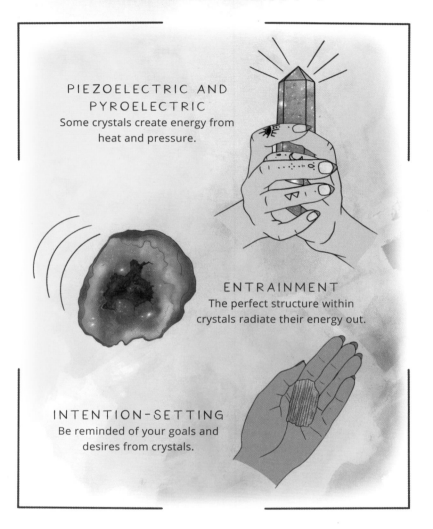

PIEZOELECTRIC AND PYROELECTRIC
Some crystals create energy from heat and pressure.

ENTRAINMENT
The perfect structure within crystals radiate their energy out.

INTENTION-SETTING
Be reminded of your goals and desires from crystals.

CHAPTER 2

EXPERIENCING CRYSTAL ENERGY

Everyone who works with crystals wants to feel something. Throughout my years working in the spiritual community as an educator and a writer, I've encountered many people who say they don't feel anything when they hold a crystal. Most of these people automatically think that because they don't feel anything, crystal energy must not be real or they're missing out on something magickal. Don't sweat it!

If you don't feel anything when you hold a crystal, even if it's supposedly the most amazing and powerful crystal in the world, then you might not be a frequency match with that crystal. That's why it's important to identify crystals that resonate with *you*, not someone else.

IDENTIFYING CRYSTALS
THAT RESONATE WITH YOU

As you embark on your crystal journey, one of the most exciting things is learning which crystals are best suited for your unique energy. You can feel more connected to a crystal because of its color, mineral content, or vibrational frequency. Working with stones that you resonate with will offer a deeper level of healing, and it is more likely that you'll be able to feel their energy.

To discover which crystals you align with, it's best to experience a variety of them. Following are some ways you can begin experimenting with different crystals.

VISIT CRYSTAL SHOPS AND MINERAL SHOWS

If you're able to go somewhere that sells a variety of crystals, like a crystal shop or a mineral show, that's great! Make sure that when you go, you have enough time to be present in the space and not feel rushed. When you enter the store or mineral show, take a few moments to connect with your breath. Notice when you feel called to a specific crystal, and honor your hunches. If you find something that has piqued your interest, ask if you can hold it. You might feel a tingling sensation in your hands or an overall positive shift in your body. I'll discuss feeling crystal energy in greater detail in the next chapter.

◂〰 EXPERIMENT WITH TUMBLED STONES 〰▸

If there aren't any crystal shops or mineral shows near you, sets of tumbled stones can be purchased for a relatively small price online. I also suggest working with tumbled stones if you're highly sensitive to the energy of other people. Working with a set of tumbled stones is a great way to experiment with a variety of crystals in the comfort of your own home.

To work with a set of tumbled stones, lay out your crystals in front of you, close your eyes, and breathe for a few minutes. Open your eyes and gaze at your tumbled stones; notice whether there are any that you feel compelled to hold. If you do, hold it in your hands and ask whether it has anything to share with you. Notice how you feel and be aware of any sensations or messages you may receive.

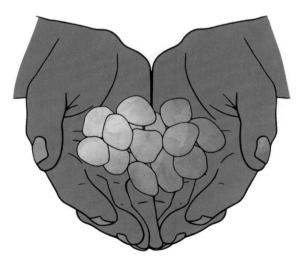

If visiting a crystal shop, mineral show, or purchasing tumbled stones aren't options for you, I suggest looking at each crystal shown in the crystal guide in the last chapter of this book. Notice which gems jump out at you. Trust that your body and spirit know what it needs and that you'll be guided to the crystals that you need the most.

If you don't feel immediately drawn to any specific crystals, that's okay! I share a variety of exercises throughout this book to experience crystal energy. It takes time to become more sensitive to energy, and everyone comes into the world with varying degrees of sensitivity. Continue to be open and curious about the energy of crystals. Eventually, you will begin to connect with their energy.

Of course, there are a few crystals that can help anyone. For example, clear quartz is beneficial for all zodiac signs, the physical body, and the entire energy body (which includes your aura and all of your chakras). If you're ever at a loss for which crystal to work with, clear quartz is your go-to.

·•ᗡ TIP ᗡ•·

Clear quartz is considered the master healing and balancing stone by many crystal practitioners, myself included.

CRYSTALS AND SENSITIVITIES

Another reason for not being able to feel crystal attunement is that people range in how sensitive they are to subtle energies. We come into this world with our own unique set of senses. Some people are highly sensitive to energy, and for them it may be effortless to feel the energy of different crystals. If you feel sensations when you hold different crystals, you might identify as an empath, a highly sensitive person, or someone with extrasensory perception (ESP).

FIVE CATEGORIES OF ESP

♦ **Clairvoyance**: Clear seeing

♦ **Clairaudience**: Clear hearing

♦ **Clairsentience**: Clear feeling

♦ **Clairtangency**: Clear touching

♦ **Claircognizance**: Clear knowing

ENERGY SURROUNDS EVERYONE AND
EVERYTHING, INCLUDING CRYSTALS.
ANYONE CAN LEARN TECHNIQUES TO
EXPERIENCE CRYSTAL ENERGY.

However, even if you can't feel the energy of a crystal, that doesn't mean you can't benefit from it. A crystal can still be working on your subtle energy field without you feeling it. You can also learn how to become more sensitive to the energy of crystals over time and then practice this skill. There are a variety of ways to increase your sensitivity to crystal energy, and I will share several with you throughout this chapter.

As you begin to work with crystals, you'll discover that you resonate with some more than others. Your body and spirit are unique; therefore, it makes sense that you would resonate with unique crystals. It is also completely normal to stop feeling connected with a crystal you used to love. As you continue to evolve, your energy frequency changes too.

Remember what I said previously about needing to be a frequency match with a crystal to feel it? As your energy frequency changes over time, you may find that you're attracted to different crystals. The energy of your crystals hasn't changed, but you have. For example, if you begin meditating regularly, you may find that you're drawn to higher vibrational crystals like amethyst and kyanite. The crystals that you're attracted to can be a helpful guide to better understand where you're at in your life.

I encourage you to try the techniques in this chapter whether or not you already feel the energy of crystals. If you already feel crystal energy, you'll be able to deepen your relationship with crystals and become even more sensitive to them. If working with energy is new for you, I encourage you to approach these exercises with an open mind.

WAYS TO USE
CRYSTAL ENERGY

RITUAL

FEELING CRYSTAL
ENERGY

PROTECTION

HEALING
DURING SLEEP

UNDERSTANDING
YOUR SOUL PATH

MEDITATION

CRYSTAL
GRIDS

CHAKRA
BALANCING

CLEANSING AND CHARGING
OTHER CRYSTALS

CRYSTAL
ELIXIRS

WEARING
CRYSTALS

INTENTION-SETTING
REMINDER

FEELING CRYSTAL ENERGY IN YOUR HANDS

Your hands play an essential role in experiencing all kinds of energy, including crystal energy. You have small, secondary chakras in the palms of your hands. You may be familiar with the body's seven primary chakras. Chakras are invisible wheels of energy that are part of your subtle body system. If the chakra system is new to you, see pages 50 to 52.

The chakras in your hands are important because they can give and receive energy. Your right and left hand each work with energy differently. Your dominant hand is your giving hand, and it is responsible for sending out energy, manifesting, and making things happen. Your giving hand is associated with yang energy, or active energy. Your nondominant hand is your receiving hand and is responsible for accepting energy, receiving gifts, and feeling. Your receiving hand is associated with yin energy, which is more passive.

As you become more adept at feeling energy in your hands, you may notice that you become more sensitive in general and, if you do, I suggest working with protective stones to help shield your energy.

·•◊ TIP ◊•·

You can utilize your receiving hand for much more than feeling crystal energy! This same technique can be applied to spiritual tools of all kinds, like oracle cards, tarot cards, and pendulums.

GIVING AND RECEIVING HANDS

RECEIVE ENERGY WITH YOUR NON-DOMINANT HAND
Yin • Accepting • Feeling

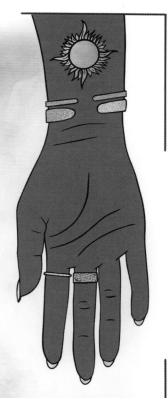

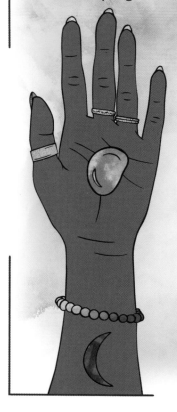

GIVE ENERGY WITH YOUR DOMINANT HAND
Yang • Expressive • Active

IDENTIFYING YOUR GIVING AND RECEIVING HANDS

For this exercise, you'll need a crystal of your choice and 5 minutes of quiet time. If you're unsure about what crystal to use, quartz is a good option. If you're very sensitive to energy, rose quartz will offer soft and subtle energy.

1. Begin by quieting your mind and centering yourself. Sit comfortably, close your eyes, and focus on the sound of your breath for a few moments.

2. Rub your hands together for about 20 seconds to activate the chakras in your hands.

3. Stop rubbing your hands together and slowly begin to separate your hands from each other.

4. You may begin to feel a warming sensation, tingling, or both in the center of your palms. These sensations are a result of the energy centers in your hands becoming activated.

5. Slowly, begin to move your hands farther apart from one another, and then closer together. You may start to feel a bit of resistance between your palms. If you feel something, it is the energy radiating out from your palms.

6. Now that you've activated the energy centers of your palms, place the crystal in your receiving hand (nondominant hand). Because this is your hand that receives and experiences energy, it's more likely that you'll be able to connect with the energy of your crystal.

7. Stay seated with your crystal for a few minutes. The way that you experience the energy of a crystal can vary significantly from person to person and crystal to crystal. You may feel something physical, like a tingling in your hand. It's also possible to see a color in your mind's eye or associate a sound with a specific crystal.

If you don't feel anything, that's okay! I encourage you to come back to this exercise for 5 minutes a day for a week. If you still don't feel anything, it might be time to try a different crystal. There are some crystals that you won't be a frequency match with, and there's nothing wrong with that. Use this technique anytime you want to feel or work with the energy of a crystal. This is also a great technique to use if you're crystal shopping at a store or gem show.

··· ◈ MEDITATING WITH CRYSTALS ◈ ···

You can use countless crystal varieties to aid your meditation practice. If you're struggling to feel the energy of crystals, meditation can assist you in opening your extrasensory abilities and becoming more sensitive to crystal energy. Meditation can also help you experience the specific healing benefits of each crystal. For example, if you feel called to find more grounding and a sense of safety in your life, you may want to work with crystals that are associated with the root chakra (see chapter 7).

REASONS TO USE CRYSTALS
IN MEDITATION

- To deepen meditation
- To feel crystal energy
- To protect, repair, or cleanse your aura

- To ground yourself
- To connect to Spirit
- To balance your chakras

GROUNDING CRYSTAL MEDITATION

Grounding can make you feel more safe and secure and less anxious. There are so many crystals in the mineral kingdom that can help with grounding. Working with a grounding stone in meditation will help amplify its healing benefits.

For this meditation, you'll need 5 to 30 minutes of uninterrupted quiet time, and any grounding crystals you'd like to use. Hematite, red jasper, and black tourmaline are great options. As you can see in the crystal guide in chapter 7, any crystal with the root chakra correspondence symbol is excellent for this meditation and will bring a sense of grounding. This meditation is best to perform sitting on the floor or directly on the earth. If this isn't an option, sitting in a chair or lying down is perfectly fine.

1. Hold your grounding crystal(s) in your receiving hand or place it on your body.

2. Close your eyes and become aware of your breath.

3. Begin to elongate your inhales and exhales.

4. Take three big belly breaths, inhaling through your nose and exhaling through your mouth.

5. Visualize your crystal emitting a red field of energy that is slowly encompassing your body and forming a shield of protection.

6. Imagine in your mind's eye that this field of energy is shielding you from negativity, protecting you, and bringing you back into alignment with the earth.

7. If this energy had a feeling, it would be heavy. Imagine that this supportive and grounding energy is gently hugging your body.

8. Imagine the red field of energy removing your fears and worries and sending them into the earth to be absorbed.

9. Stay in the meditation for as long as you'd like.

10. As you end the meditation, thank your crystal and the earth for the grounding energy.

CRYSTALS FOR YOUR SOUL PATH

There are so many crystals that can help you connect with your higher self and to understand why you're here and what your purpose is during this lifetime. Any crystal that corresponds to your crown chakra, and especially your soul star chakra, will aid you in discovering your soul path. See the list of crystals below for some good options.

CRYSTALS TO HELP YOU UNDERSTAND YOUR PURPOSE

- ◆ Apophyllite
- ◆ Celestite
- ◆ Moldavite
- ◆ Selenite
- ◆ Spirit quartz
- ◆ Sugilite

SUGGESTIONS FOR WORKING WITH
HIGH-VIBRATIONAL STONES

The stones associated with the crown and soul star chakras vibrate at a very high frequency. The high frequencies of these crystals may feel overwhelming and intense. I've always felt drawn to these high-vibrational stones, but practice caution when working with them. Here are some suggestions:

♦ Work with them for short amounts of time.

♦ Work with them under the guidance of a trained healer.

♦ Pair them with a grounding stone like hematite or moss agate.

♦ Call on angels or spirit guides to assist you in your work.

♦ Don't wear them for prolonged periods of time.

As you meditate with these high-vibrational stones, you can ask the crystal to share more about your purpose with you. Likewise, if you're struggling with something specific, you can ask the crystal about it as well. Your higher self will be able to shed light on anything you need help with, and these high-vibrational stones can help connect you to your higher self.

HIGH-VIBRATIONAL STONES WILL HELP YOU ALIGN WITH YOUR TRUE CALLING.

CRYSTALS ON THE BODY

Placing crystals directly on the body is another way to enjoy their healing properties and connect to their energy. Every crystal corresponds with a chakra, and every chakra corresponds to a part of your body. Understanding the chakra system will help you better understand crystal energy and enable you to work with crystals in a more meaningful way. See all seven chakras on the next page.

Crystal energy affects our subtle body systems. Among other things, your subtle body system is comprised of your chakras and your aura. For this reason, I believe the chakras are an integral part of working with crystals. I also share the chakras that each crystal corresponds to in pages 140 to 155.

To allow crystal energy to work with your physical and subtle body in this way, simply lie down, place your stone on the coordinating body part, close your eyes, and rest. You might feel something or you might not—either is fine. Spend as much time as you'd like with the crystal.

To dive even deeper into this technique, you can place crystal grids on the body. Use any of the crystal grids outlined in pages 126 to 135. I suggest working with a friend or loved one to assist with placing crystal grids on the body.

···◈ THE CHAKRA SYSTEM ◈···

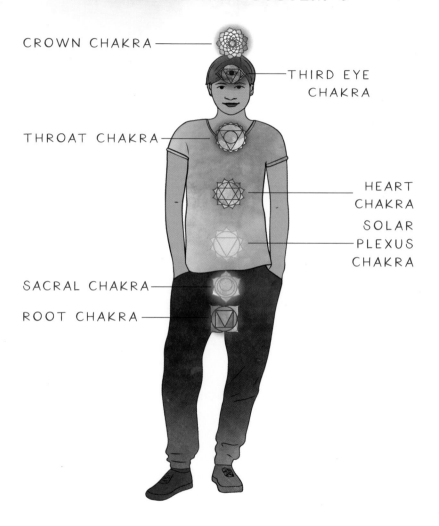

CROWN CHAKRA

THIRD EYE CHAKRA

THROAT CHAKRA

HEART CHAKRA

SOLAR PLEXUS CHAKRA

SACRAL CHAKRA

ROOT CHAKRA

WHERE TO PLACE CRYSTALS FOR DIFFERENT PURPOSES

- **Crown chakra for spiritual guidance**: Celestite or howlite on the forehead.

- **Third eye chakra for intuition**: Amethyst or kyanite in between the eyebrows.

- **Throat chakra for speaking your truth**: Lapis lazuli or chrysocolla on the throat.

- **Heart chakra for love**: Rose quartz or kunzite on the heart.

- **Solar plexus chakra for willpower**: Pyrite or yellow jasper on the stomach.

- **Sacral chakra for creativity**: Carnelian or rainbow moonstone on the low belly.

- **Root chakra for Grounding**: Red jasper or hematite on the pubic bone.

···◈ CRYSTAL ELIXIRS ◈···

Crystal and gem elixirs have become trendy in the crystal community. It's an important subject to discuss because there's a great deal of misinformation about this topic that can affect your health.

> ### ·◦ TIP ◦·
>
> **Some crystals are toxic if ingested, so I suggest creating crystal elixirs using an indirect soaking method. I also suggest speaking to your health care provider before ingesting anything.**

Crystal elixirs are created by soaking a crystal directly or indirectly in water or some other kind of solution for a prolonged period of time. The energy of the crystal is infused into the liquid, which you can then consume. You can even find crystal water bottles on the market! Crystal elixirs are a powerful tool, but only if you create them safely. Several crystals can be toxic if ingested; a quick internet search will provide you with a list of crystals that you shouldn't ingest.

To avoid the risk of ingesting anything toxic, I suggest creating the elixirs using an indirect soaking method. To do this, place your crystal in a glass vessel and then place that vessel into your water. Because crystals radiate their energy outward, your water doesn't need to touch the crystal. Water is highly impressionable to energy, and it will still be harmonized by your crystal, even if it's not directly contacting it.

AMPLIFY YOUR INTUITION CRYSTAL ELIXIR

You'll need:

- ♦ A glass bowl
- ♦ 8 ounces (240 ml) of water (less or more is okay)
- ♦ Amethyst (any shape or amount will do)
- ♦ A glass vial or cup that can fit inside your bowl
- ♦ Full moon

1. Fill your larger bowl with about 8 ounces (240 ml) of water.

2. Place your amethyst in your smaller vial or cup.

3. Place the vial or cup with the amethyst inside the bowl. Do this in a way that the water isn't touching the amethyst.

4. Place the bowl under the light of a full moon.

5. Leave the bowl for the entire night.

6. Pour the water into a bottle and seal. Drink the water anytime you'd like to enhance your intuition.

Note: Crystal elixirs can be kept in a sealed container in the refrigerator for a few days but should be used quickly.

CRYSTAL HEALING
WHILE YOU SLEEP

An easy and effective way to work with crystal energy is while you sleep! Working with crystals in this way takes all the pressure off of needing to feel something as you work with the crystal because you'll be fast asleep. The crystal energy can slowly work on you while you dream. This is a great way to make significant shifts over time.

> ### ·•◊ TIP ◊•·
> **Avoid placing energizing stones like citrine, carnelian, or pyrite around you while you sleep. Crystals with solar plexus or sacral chakra correspondences are energizing.**

Placing crystals near you as you sleep can help you sleep deeper, experience better dream recall, become more balanced, and help you receive intuitive guidance. There are a variety of crystals that you can work with while you sleep, many of which I've outlined in chapter 7. If you're ever in doubt about which stone to place on your nightstand, amethyst is always a good choice. Amethyst can help you receive intuitive messages in your dreams and will protect you from nightmares.

CRYSTALS FOR HEALING WHILE YOU SLEEP

- ◆ **Sleep deeper**: Amethyst, howlite, or blue lace agate
- ◆ **Lucid dreaming**: Amethyst or moonstone
- ◆ **Nightmare protection**: Amethyst, lepidolite, or smoky quartz
- ◆ **Receive intuitive messages as you sleep**: Amethyst or labradorite

WHERE TO PLACE CRYSTALS

- ◆ On your nightstand
- ◆ Under your pillow
- ◆ Under your mattress

CRYSTALS IN RITUAL AND MAGICK WORK

Crystals and magick work go hand in hand! Ritual and magick work is where the knowledge of correspondences comes in handy. Every crystal carries a unique energy signature based off of its color and unique makeup. The energy signature of each crystal corresponds, or aligns, with symbols and tools that carry a similar energy. Crystals and tools that correspond with each other can be combined to amplify the intention of your magick work.

For example, if you would like to invite more abundance into your life and want to perform an abundance spell, you might want to work with pyrite. Pyrite is associated with the waxing crescent moon phase, which is all about growth and expansion. Working with pyrite during the first quarter moon will be more beneficial because you're in alignment with the phase of the moon that is offering the same kind of energy as the pyrite. You can continue to add to your intention with other tools and symbols that are in alignment, or correspond, with the energy of abundance. Learn how to set up your own abundance altar with the exercise on pages 62 to 63.

The abundance altar is just one suggestion, but you can use crystals in this way for any purpose! Crystals are an excellent addition to charm bags (spells in a bag), spell bottles, altars, and candle magick. The crystal guide in this book provides lunar, astrological, and chakra correspondences to help you pair the right crystals with all of your magickal practices.

Beyond amplifying your magickal practices, crystals are used to create a variety of magickal tools. Crystals are often used for pendulums, which are a pointed crystal on the end of a string or chain used as a divination tool. More recently you can find athames (ritual knives) crafted from different crystals. Additionally, one of the most popular magickal tools for divination is also the crystal ball!

Crystal ball gazing is part of a larger psychic practice referred to as scrying. Scrying is the act of perceiving psychic visions in a reflective surface like a bowl of water, the moon, a mirror, or a crystal ball. Even though it's common to see clear quartz crystal balls used in this way, crystal ball gazing can be performed with a variety of different crystals. Use your intuition to select a crystal ball for your scrying practice and check out pages 64 to 65 for getting started.

CRYSTALS FOR ENERGY PROTECTION

Anytime you come into contact with other people, you have the opportunity to feel and absorb their energy. Being around negative energy regularly can be extremely draining and may even shift your mood to one of negativity.

There are so many crystals that can help shield you from negative energy and cleanse negative energy from your subtle body. If you live in a busy city or work at a job that requires you to be around a lot of people, I suggest wearing or carrying a protective crystal. If you feel like you need energetic protection where you live, there are solutions for that as well.

On page 132, I share a protection crystal grid. This grid is great for protecting the energy of your home or office. Even if you don't have all of the crystals for the protection crystal grid, you can place any of the protective crystals outlined in chapter 7 around your space. Any crystal that corresponds with the root chakra will also offer protection.

Crystal energy can be utilized in every facet of your life because crystals correspond to all different kinds of energy. Each of the exercises in this chapter can be adapted to receive different kinds of crystal energies. I hope they spark a feeling of creativity and exploration within you to experience crystal energy in new ways.

PROTECTIVE CRYSTALS

♦ **Amethyst**: Transmutes negativity into love

♦ **Black tourmaline**: Deflects and clears negative energy

♦ **Hematite**: Blocks negative energy

♦ **Labradorite**: Shields and repairs the aura

♦ **Smoky quartz**: Grounds you to the earth to help absorb unwanted energy

ABUNDANCE ALTAR

You'll need:

- ◆ Waxing moon phase (any moon phase from the new moon to the full moon)

- ◆ Green aventurine

- ◆ Pyrite

- ◆ Fehu rune symbol

- ◆ Paper money

- ◆ A space to put your altar

- ◆ Green candle

1. During any waxing moon phase, place the green aventurine, pyrite, fehu rune symbol, and money somewhere you'll see them regularly. Place your items in any arrangement that feels good to you. This will be your altar.

2. Light your green candle. Green corresponds to growth, so it is the ideal color to work with when asking for abundance and wealth.

3. Hold each item in your hand and visualize what you are trying to bring more of into your life.

4. Imagine how you'll feel when you have more of what you're trying to manifest.

5. If you can, stay with your altar until the candle burns through. If you're using a larger candle, snuff out the candle rather than blowing it out.

6. Try to make contact with your abundance altar every day that it is up. Leave your abundance altar up until the full moon.

CRYSTAL BALL GAZING

You'll need some quiet time, a crystal ball, and a journal can be handy as well. Scrying is a deep and rich practice; if you enjoy this activity, I encourage you to dive deeper into the art of scrying!

1. Cleanse your crystal ball with any technique mentioned in chapter 3.

2. Ensure that you have 30 to 60 minutes of uninterrupted time to perform your crystal ball gazing. Scrying work is best performed at night.

3. Candlelight or moonlight is ideal for crystal ball gazing. Situate yourself so that you have access to moonlight, or light a candle.

4. Call on any guides, spirits, or ancestors you may work with to aid and protect you. You can optionally add some protective stones to your space as you work.

5. Get quiet and spend 2 to 3 minutes connecting with your breath.

6. If you're focusing on a specific question, ask it now, either aloud or in your mind. You don't have to ask a question and can simply allow things to come to you.

7. Begin to gaze into your crystal. If it is translucent, you can gaze into the ball. If your crystal ball is not translucent, observe the patterns of light and shadow on the outside of the sphere.

8. Soften your gaze and allow your mind to go where it wants.

9. Allow yourself to become immersed in the crystal ball, you may even feel like you've entered a trance state.

10. You may experience seeing visions in or on the crystal, or in your mind's eye.

11. When you feel like you're ready to end your crystal gazing session, give yourself time to come out of it slowly.

12. Thank any guides, ancestors, or spirits you may have called on. Write anything you experienced down in your journal so you can remember later.

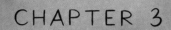

CHAPTER 3

CLEANSING CRYSTALS

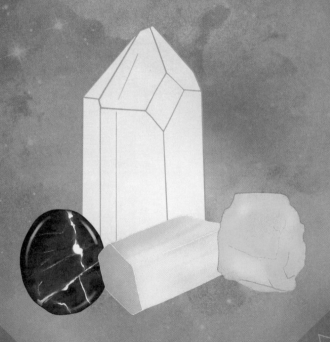

E ven though crystals are extremely stable structures, over time they can pick up energy from their environment and the people around them. It's also possible that any crystal you purchase could have been previously programmed, resulting in it carrying an energy you don't desire. This is especially true for crystals in the quartz family, which are masters when it comes to storing information. Most minerals can store information, so this is relevant to any crystal you're working with, but doubly important for crystals in the quartz family.

If a crystal was previously owned by someone who was extremely negative, it might be storing some of their residual negative energy. Have you ever held a crystal that you needed to put down right away because it just didn't feel right? Or have you picked up a crystal that you knew you needed in your life because of the way it felt? Much of how you feel about a crystal has to do with the energy frequency it's emitting. Still, the energy it has collected over its life will affect it as well.

Let's think about all of the humans your crystal may come in contact with if you purchased one at a store or online. First, the crystal is mined out of the earth. From the mining process, it will eventually find its way to a lapidary company, where it is cut, formed, and polished. Next, the stones will usually be sold to a wholesale company, which then sells it to retailers. This list doesn't even include all of the possible travel time your gemstone had and postal workers that may have handled it. Hundreds of people may have handled a crystal you pick up at a store. That is a lot of different energy!

CLEANSE AWAY NEGATIVE ENERGY TO MAKE SPACE FOR GROWTH AND GIFTS.

Because crystals can come in contact with so much energy between being mined and being purchased, it's another reason to know the source of your crystals. If you're able to mine your own crystals or get them directly from a miner, that's ideal, but not possible for most. The next best option is to know your sources— the fewer steps your crystal had to go through to get to you, the better. Finding crystals close to their source is useful for a variety of reasons, from the energy your stone picks up to its overall carbon footprint.

WHEN TO CLEANSE YOUR CRYSTALS

Because crystals pick up the energy around them, it's essential to cleanse them. Knowing when to cleanse your crystals can be based on your intuition or when specific events happen, such as:

♦ You purchase a new crystal

♦ Other people have handled a crystal

♦ You use your crystal regularly

♦ You've been ill and have been working with a specific crystal

♦ The crystal was programmed for an intention that is no longer needed or has been completed

♦ You experience a substantial mental or spiritual experience while holding or carrying a specific crystal

Now that you have a better idea of why and when you should cleanse your crystals, let's dive into some techniques for doing so.

CLEANSING VERSUS CHARGING CRYSTALS

Before we go on, I want to clear up any confusion you might have about the difference between cleansing and charging crystals, because they're two distinct things. See the list on the next page to better understand the differences between cleansing and charging.

To make the topic of cleansing and charging a little more confusing, some crystal cleansing techniques will also charge crystals. There are still differences between cleansing and charging, even if you're using the same method. The difference will lie in your intentions. For example, if you're cleansing and charging your crystals with your energy, you'll have a different intent for each one.

Now, let's dive into the ways to cleanse your precious crystals! You can perform more than one cleansing technique on your crystals. If you're planning to cleanse several crystals at once, it can be fun to perform a cleansing ritual by cleansing yourself, your space, and your crystals with a variety of cleansing techniques. That said, it's also fine to perform a quick crystal cleanse on a new stone you recently purchased. The most important thing is that you're cleansing them!

THE DIFFERENCES BETWEEN CLEANSING AND CHARGING CRYSTALS

CLEANSING CRYSTALS

- Removes energy

- Cleanses imprinted energy from previous charging or programming

- Restores crystal to its natural state

CHARGING CRYSTALS

- Adds specific energy

- Energizes the crystal

- Imparts specific energy depending on the charging method

CRYSTAL CLEANSING TECHNIQUES

There's no excuse to skip cleansing your crystals, because there are so many ways to do it. There are a few cleansing techniques that you'll be able to perform without any additional tools. Some require tools, but they're all relatively easy to come by, and you might even have some of them in your home already.

> ·◦◊ TIP ◁◦·
>
> **Any technique you use to cleanse your crystals will also cleanse your energy!**

I suggest trying as many of these techniques as you can to determine which ones work the best for you and your crystals. You may find that you have specific crystals that have cleansing preferences. Keep an open mind and listen to your intuition!

WAYS TO CLEANSE CRYSTALS

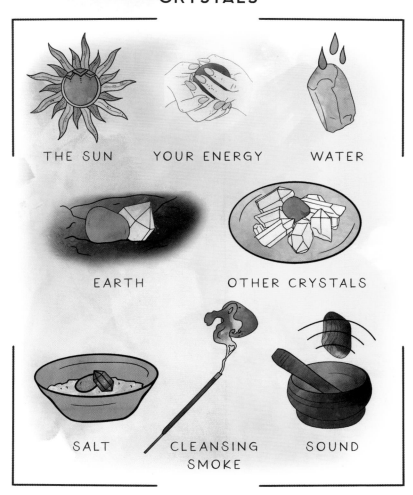

THE SUN   YOUR ENERGY   WATER

EARTH   OTHER CRYSTALS

SALT   CLEANSING SMOKE   SOUND

···✧ CLEANSING WITH THE SUN ✧···

Our bright sun offers a potent and efficient crystal cleanse. Place your crystals outside at midday for about 30 minutes to enjoy optimal cleansing benefits from the sun. If you live in a warm climate, be careful, as your crystals might heat up quickly and be hot to the touch.

Some crystals can lose their color over time if left out in the sun for prolonged periods. A short crystal cleanse now and then will usually be fine.

CRYSTALS THAT SHOULD AVOID PROLONGED SUN EXPOSURE

- ♦ Amethyst
- ♦ Ametrine
- ♦ Aquamarine
- ♦ Celestite
- ♦ Citrine
- ♦ Fluorite
- ♦ Opal
- ♦ Rose quartz
- ♦ Sapphire
- ♦ Smoky quartz
- ♦ Topaz

···◆ CLEANSING WITH SOUND ◆···

Sound is a strong healing tool, not only for crystals but for humans too. Sound is one of my favorite cleansing techniques because it is a vibration. Sound causes the air molecules to vibrate around it, and they continue to ripple out into the environment. Because we're all energy, vibrating at different frequencies, the vibration of sound will help remove any unwanted energy from your crystals.

SOUND SENDS VIBRATIONAL FREQUENCIES THROUGH YOUR CRYSTALS, BRINGING THEM BACK INTO THEIR NATURAL ALIGNMENT.

For each of the sound cleansing techniques listed on pages 76 to 77, lay or hold your crystals near the source of the sound. Each of your crystals must bathe in the sound waves to be cleansed. If you're just cleansing a few crystals, you can also opt to hold each crystal directly in the path of the sound. However, if you're using a singing bowl, don't place your crystals directly in the bowl, as this could affect the sound it makes.

SOUND CLEANSING TECHNIQUES

CHANTING OM

Chanting is a free way to cleanse your crystals with sound. To do this, prepare your crystals, inhale deep into your belly, and release a loud OOOMMMMMM sound that can encompass your crystals. I recommend chanting for 2 to 5 minutes.

·ᴐ TIP ᴐ·

If you're new to chanting OM, do an online search for a video to ensure that you're pronouncing it correctly. Pronouncing OM correctly will make it a stronger cleanser.

SINGING BOWLS

Singing bowls can be found in glass, metal, and crystal. They vary significantly in price. Most singing bowls emit a loud enough sound that you can just have your crystals near the bowl to cleanse them. If you decide to invest in a singing bowl, it can be used for a variety of purposes beyond cleansing your crystals, such as healing, stress relief, and meditation.

TUNING FORKS

Tuning forks may not be as readily available in local stores, but can be found easily online. Tuning forks aren't massive, so they make great portable crystal cleansers! The sound emitted from a tuning fork won't seem loud, unless you hold it up to your ear. You'll need to strike the tuning fork and move it around each of your crystals to cleanse them properly. Similar to singing bowls, tuning forks can be used for other healing purposes.

CHIMES AND GONGS

Chimes and gongs can both be used to cleanse crystals but may be harder to find for a reasonable price. Large gongs make excellent crystal cleansers because their sound is so loud and sustained. If you're able to attend an event with a gong, and it's appropriate to bring some crystals, I'd take advantage of it!

CLEANSING WITH OTHER CRYSTALS

Using other crystals to cleanse your crystals might sound counterintuitive, but there are a handful of crystals that make great cleansers! My favorite thing about using other crystals to cleanse my crystals is that it's easy to do and attractive looking. That said, this can be one of the more expensive techniques for cleansing crystals. Here are my crystal cleansing techniques and their suggested uses.

As I've mentioned, clear quartz is a master healer and balancer. Place a large, cleansed, clear quartz near any smaller stones for 3 to 5 hours to cleanse them and bring them back into harmony.

Amethyst is in the quartz family and transmutes negative energy. It has long been used as a tool to cleanse and protect. Amethyst geodes make excellent healing tools because of all of their points, which direct their energy outward. You'll need an amethyst geode that's large enough to put your crystals on or inside it. Place your crystals on or inside the geode for a few hours or overnight.

Selenite has a very high vibration, which makes it an ideal cleanser for other crystals and objects. You can find selenite in a variety of shapes, but a selenite plate or wand are best for cleansing. To cleanse crystals with selenite you can set them on top of the selenite or wave a selenite wand around the crystal your cleansing for 1 to 2 minutes. Selenite is a very cleansing and high-vibrational stone, and will cleanse your crystals quickly. The beautiful thing about a selenite plate is that you can use it to cleanse anything you can fit on the selenite. I like to use my selenite plate to place my cup of water or tea on.

HOW TO CLEANSE YOUR ···◈ CRYSTALS WITH OTHER ◈··· CRYSTALS

LARGE CLEAR QUARTZ

AMETHYST GEODE

SELENITE PLATE

CLEANSING WITH YOUR ENERGY

If you're looking for a free way to cleanse your crystals, look no further! You can cleanse your lovely crystals with your energy alone. Your subtle energy body, which, among other things, includes your chakras and aura, emits an energy frequency that can be used to cleanse your crystals. You may also see this referred to as Reiki cleansing. You don't have to be trained as a Reiki practitioner to use this cleansing technique. You can also tune in to the spirit world to call forth energy from the other side to cleanse your crystals.

If this technique sounds a little too "out there" for you, I encourage you to keep an open mind and try it. You don't have to use it as your primary crystal cleansing method, but you might have some crystals that enjoy it!

CLEANSING CRYSTALS WITH YOUR ENERGY

1. Block out 5 to 30 minutes (depending on how many crystals you have) and lay your crystals out in front of you.

2. Spend a few minutes focusing on your breath and centering yourself.

3. Meditate for 2 to 3 minutes. As you meditate, visualize a stream of bright white light coming down from the sky, through the crown of your head and your hands.

4. Hold a crystal in your hands and visualize the white cleansing light from above, removing any negative energy and restoring the crystal to a perfectly balanced state.

5. If you'd like, you can call on any loved ones passed on, angels, guides, gods, or goddesses to help you cleanse the crystal.

6. Hold your crystal as long as you feel you need to cleanse it fully.

7. Thank any spiritual aids you called on for their help and place the crystal back down.

8. Repeat steps 4 to 7 for any remaining crystals you'd like to cleanse.

···◆ SMOKE CLEANSING ◆···

The smoke of dried plants and resins has been used by cultures around the world to cleanse and protect. You can use this technique to cleanse your crystals, your environment, and yourself.

To perform a smoke cleanse for your crystals, use any of the herbs, resins, or incense listed on the follwing page. Once you've decided on a smoke to work with, light it in a fireproof dish or abalone shell. Hold your crystals in the smoke or waft the smoke around your crystals for 2 to 3 minutes.

Note: As with any work that utilizes smoke and fire, you must have the correct tools and safety precautions in place beforehand. Use fire-safe dishes for herb and resin burning, never leave burning herbs or resins unattended, and always ensure proper ventilation and fire safety.

·◦◦ TIP ◦◦·

White sage is a common and popular plant to use for cleansing, but I encourage you to try some alternatives! White sage is often overharvested, and oftentimes unethically. Furthermore, white sage is a sacred plant for many indigenous people, so it must be used with the utmost respect. If you decide that white sage is the best option for your crystal cleansing, try to purchase it from a sustainable company that grows their own.

CLEANSING HERBS, RESINS, AND INCENSE

CEDAR   MUGWORT   GARDEN SAGE   JUNIPER

ROSEMARY   LAVENDER   DESERT SAGE

FRANKINCENSE   COPAL   MYRRH

CLEANSING WITH SALT AND WATER

Salt and water can be used together or separately as a cleansing tool. Some crystals aren't suitable for water and/or salt, which can be harsh and abrasive for stones that are low on the Mohs hardness scale. This can cause them to lose their luster.

Any kind of salt can be used in its natural and dry state to cleanse your crystals. Simply place your crystals in a tray or bowl of salt and leave them there for 4 to 5 hours, and overnight is even better.

If you decide to cleanse your crystals in water alone, natural running water is always ideal. If you're lucky enough to live near a natural spring, river, ocean, or waterfall, these are the best options for cleansing your crystals with water. If you're not near a body of natural water, tap water will work, but you'll need to hold your crystal in it for a longer time. For natural bodies of water, hold your crystal in a moving current for a minute or longer. For tap water, hold your crystal under running water for 3 to 5 minutes. You can also place your crystals in a bowl of natural or tap water overnight, although running natural water is always best.

·•◇ TIP ◇•·

Water has a special relationship with the moon. To amplify the moon's crystal charging abilities, and to cleanse your crystals, place them in a bowl of water under the light of the moon.

Lastly, you can combine the power of salt and water for a saltwater cleanse. If you live near an ocean, you can take saltwater straight from the sea! Otherwise, a mixture of any kind of salt and spring water will work. Place your crystals in a bowl of saltwater overnight.

CRYSTALS THAT SHOULD AVOID WATER

- Amber
- Ammolite
- Angelite
- Azurite
- Calcite
- Celestite
- Charoite
- Chrysocolla
- Fluorite
- Halite
- Hematite
- Jet
- Larimar
- Magnetite
- Malachite
- Opal
- Rhodochrosite
- Selenite

CRYSTALS THAT SHOULD AVOID SALT

- Amber
- Emerald
- Onyx
- Opal
- Turquoise

···◈ CLEANSING WITH THE EARTH ◈···

Your crystals were forged within the earth, so it's not a surprise that they can be cleansed by returning to their cozy home. Aside from your crystals being comfortable with earth energy, it also offers potent cleansing.

The electromagnetic field of the earth and negative ions that it emits will help restore your crystals to their original state and remove any negative energy. To cleanse your crystals with the earth, bury your crystals in some dirt or sand. Leave your crystals there for 3 to 5 days.

·◦ᴅ TIP ᴅ◦·

Cleansing your crystals in the earth will impart potent grounding energy to your crystals. It's an ideal method if you feel like you need to be more grounded.

As I've mentioned earlier, there are a multitude of techniques for restoring your crystals and cleansing them of any unwanted energy. You may find that specific crystals prefer specific cleaning methods. Try to rely on your intuition when determining cleansing techniques for your crystals.

ENERGY IS CONTAGIOUS.
SURROUND YOURSELF
WITH THE KIND OF
ENERGY YOU WANT TO
PUT INTO THE WORLD.

CHAPTER 4

CHARGING CRYSTALS

O nce you've cleansed the energy from your crystals, they're ready for charging. Charging a crystal is the act of adding specific energy to it and amplifying the crystal's innate energy. You'll find that some of the techniques I share for charging crystals are the same as for cleansing. Some tools work for both cleansing and charging.

As you work with your crystals, their energy will fade over time, which is why you may want to charge them. Another reason for charging is if you're planning to use a crystal for a specific purpose. Charging your crystals is important but not as necessary as cleansing them. You may have crystals that you feel don't need charging, and that's okay! Charging your crystals is most helpful when you plan to work with them for a specific purpose or you need an extra push of energy to accomplish your goals.

CHARGING A CRYSTAL AMPLIFIES ITS ENERGY.

How you charge a crystal will depend entirely on how you intend to use it. Charging differs from cleansing crystals in this way. For the most part, it's fine to cleanse all of your crystals at once. On the other hand, it is best to charge your crystals individually so you can impart the proper intention on each crystal.

WHEN TO CHARGE YOUR CRYSTALS

- ♦ After they've been cleansed

- ♦ When you want to energize your crystals

- ♦ After using it for a specific purpose for more than a month (or sooner if you feel you should)

- ♦ If you're using a crystal for a new intention

- ♦ To unify the energy of a variety of crystals for a grid

CRYSTAL CHARGING TECHNIQUES

I often hear people say, "I put all of my crystals out for the full moon last night!" The full moon brings a very specific kind of energy and you might not want all of your crystals to be charged with the intense energy of the full moon. The full moon brings an energy of heightened intuition, fulfillment, and celebration. These are all lovely things, but if you're working with a crystal to help lessen your anxiety and bring more calming energy into your life, the full moon isn't the best option for charging. In a situation like this, you may opt to charge your crystals under a waning or dark moon phase. You'll likely only need to charge a few select crystals in the light of the full moon. Use your intuition while charging your crystals.

Charging is all about imparting specific energy into your crystal. If you feel called to charge your crystals in a way that isn't outlined here, like in the ocean, please do so! Crystals are receptive to the energy you send to them, which can be done in so many ways. As long as the energy you're sending to your crystal matches your intention, there's no wrong way to charge your crystals.

·◦◇ TIP ◇◦·

Always cleanse your crystals before charging them.

I'm going to share four different crystal charging techniques with you and the reasons why you may want to use each technique. As I mentioned, some cleansing and charging techniques overlap, like the sun. Using a charging method that also cleanses can be helpful when you want to cleanse and charge a crystal quickly.

Two common ways to charge crystals are with the sun and the moon. One way to understand the difference between lunar and solar energy is through yin and yang. The moon offers yin energy, and the sun offers yang energy.

Charging your crystals is a powerful way to deepen the intention behind the crystals you're using. I think you'll find that working with the sun and moon in this way will also bring you into better alignment with nature. Crystals are born within the earth, and it creates a beautiful trinity of energy to charge and cleanse them with the sun and moon.

···✦ YIN AND YANG ENERGY ✦···

Yin energy from the moon is:

◆ Passive

◆ Feminine

◆ Restful

◆ Calm

◆ Intuitive

◆ Slow

Yang energy from the sun is:

◆ Active

◆ Masculine

◆ Energetic

◆ Loud

◆ Logical

◆ Fast

···✦ CHARGING WITH SUNLIGHT ✦···

Our amazing, life-giving sun can both cleanse and charge your crystals. What a gift! As with cleansing, make sure that the crystals you place in the sun won't fade or be damaged. See the list of stones that should avoid prolonged sun exposure on page 74. That said, if you're only placing your crystal in the sunlight for 30 minutes or in the light of the rising or setting sun, it will probably be okay.

Unlike cleansing your crystals, you might find that the energy of the rising or setting sun is more appropriate for charging. For cleansing purposes, the light of the midday sun works well, because it is a strong and efficient cleanser. Softer and less harsh sunlight may be more appropriate for charging. Use your intuition, and do what feels best to you.

> ·•◁ TIP ▷•·
>
> Some crystals, especially clear quartz spheres, can amplify the heat of the sun. Be careful not to place your crystals near something that could catch fire!

To charge your crystals in sunlight, place them in the light of the sun for 30 minutes to an hour. When you finish charging your crystals in the sunlight, don't touch them for a while, as the sun can heat them quickly!

CHARGING WITH THE SUN

Charge crystals with the power of the sun when you want to increase:

- ◆ Abundance
- ◆ Confidence
- ◆ Energy

- ◆ Leadership
- ◆ Luck
- ◆ Manifesting

- ◆ Protection
- ◆ Stamina
- ◆ Willpower

CHARGING WITH MOONLIGHT

The moon has long been associated with all things magickal and mystical. It's no surprise that it has become a popular tool for charging crystals. As you can see from the diagram on page 93, the overall attributes of lunar energy are passive and feminine. But the moon is unique because it goes through phases, and each moon phase brings a different kind of energy.

Though the moon is generally associated with less intense energy than the sun, that doesn't mean it isn't powerful. After trying different charging techniques, you may discover that you prefer the energy of the moon over the sun. You can find a moon phase for just about any kind of energy you need for charging crystals.

BE IN FLOW WITH THE PHASES OF THE MOON.

To charge your crystals in moonlight, first decide which moon phase best suits your needs. See page 99 to learn what kind of energy each phase will impart to your crystals. Once you've selected the best moon phase for your crystal, place it under the light of the moon, where it will receive some extra energy from Mother Earth too, or on a window sill. Because the lunar energy is less intense and totally safe for your crystals, you can leave your crystals in the moonlight for an entire night.

Before we dive into the energy associated with each moon phase, I want to share a little bit about understanding the cycles of the moon. Learning more about the order of the moon phases will not only help you be more in tune with the moon, but it will also make the energy associated with each phase make more sense.

Every moon phase begins with a new moon. As the light of the moon increases, it becomes the waxing moon phase. When we break down the waxing moon phase, it includes the waxing crescent, first quarter moon, and the waxing gibbous. The full moon happens in the middle of the lunar cycle when the moon is at its fullest and reflecting the most light from the sun. After the full moon, when the moon begins to decrease in light, the waning moon phase begins. The waning moon phase includes the waning gibbous, last quarter moon, and the waning crescent. When the moon is in conjunction with the sun (in between the earth and the sun), it isn't visible in the sky; this is the time of the dark moon phase.

There are differing opinions about when the new moon happens and if the dark moon is a true lunar phase. Most astrologers and astronomers consider the dark moon phase the new moon. For most Wiccans, Pagans, and practicing Witches, the new moon happens right after the dark moon when the moon shows the tiniest sliver of light. Both options are correct; it's a matter of what feels better to you! I have chosen to include the dark moon phase in this book because I honor it in my practice.

CHARGING WITH THE MOON

Charge crystals with the power of the moon when you want to increase:

- Acceptance
- Creativity
- Dreams
- Healing
- Intuition
- Love
- Psychic abilities
- Relationships
- Sleep

ENERGY ASSOCIATED
WITH EACH MOON PHASE

NEW
MOON
**New beginnings
and hope**

WAXING
CRESCENT
**Action and
assertion**

FIRST
QUARTER
**Focus and
momentum**

WAXING
GIBBOUS
**Refinement and
transformation**

FULL
MOON
**Intuition and
celebration**

WANING
GIBBOUS
**Reflection and
receiving**

LAST
QUARTER
**Vulnerability and
release**

WANING
CRESCENT
**Acceptance and
allowance**

DARK
MOON
**Rest and
observation**

CHARGING CRYSTALS WITH YOUR HANDS

Tap into your internal heat and energy to charge your crystals with your hands. You can use any energy you'd like to call upon to charge your crystals with your hands. Beyond imparting your crystals with energy, many believe the warmth of your body will also charge your crystals. As I mentioned in chapter 1, several crystals are pyroelectric and piezoelectric, which means they can produce energy when pressure is applied or they're heated. This reaction within your crystal will give it a quick boost of energy.

·◦◁ TIP ◁◦·

Charging crystals with your hands is a quick way to charge them before placing them on a grid or the body.

Unlike cleansing crystals, when you may have several crystals you're cleansing at once, you'll probably only have a few that need charging. Before you begin charging your crystals, rub your hands together to warm them up and activate the energy centers in the palms of your hands. Place each crystal in your hands, one at a time. Rub each crystal in between your palms for 10 to 30 seconds. That's it! Place your charged crystal directly on the body or in the grid you're using.

CHARGING CRYSTALS WITH OTHER CRYSTALS

Crystals are another tool that can both cleanse and charge. Not all of the crystals you'd use for cleansing are ideal for charging. I suggest using a geode-type crystal or any crystal with several natural points for charging. Crystals with several points radiate their energy out of each of their points, which will send amplified energy into any crystal you're charging. Amethyst, quartz, or citrine geodes work well for this purpose. Alternatively, if you have several clear quartz points, you can place them in a bowl and then place the crystals you want to charge on top of them. Large geodes are a costly investment; using several quartz points is a less expensive option.

CHARGING WITH QUARTZ

♦ Place several smaller quartz points in a bowl or vessel of some kind.

♦ Set the crystals you wish to charge on top of the quartz points.

♦ Leave them on the quartz for 3 to 5 hours.

CHAPTER 5

PROGRAMMING CRYSTALS

The difference between charging and programming crystals is subtle but important. Think of charging crystals as an all-inclusive tool, whereas programming is very specific. If you want to quickly give several of your crystals a boost, charging them in sunlight or moonlight is the best option. When you want to work with a specific crystal to help you manifest a new job, for example, programming is ideal. Charging amplifies and adds energy to the crystal. Programming imprints a specific desire or intent into the crystal.

You don't have to program your crystals to benefit from them! Think of crystal programming as extra credit. Programming can help perform intense healing and manifesting, but an unprogrammed crystal will still offer energetic healing.

·◦◊ TIP ◁◦·

Save programming for crystals you're working with for particular purposes.

Programming also differs from charging in that there's only one way to program a crystal. In contrast, charging can be performed in a few different ways. To program a crystal, you'll need some time and your crystal. You'll be using your focused energy and visualization to program a crystal. Working with programmed crystals is powerful and can assist you in accomplishing your desires more quickly. The best way to work with programmed crystals is to interact with them often.

Because crystals are made of a perfectly repeated crystalline lattice, they're great at storing information. Here is a list for ideas of when you might want to program a crystal:

♦ Manifesting specific things in your life

♦ Healing parts of the body or the subtle body

♦ Working with crystals for protection

♦ Bringing specific energy into your life

HOW TO WORK WITH YOUR PROGRAMMED CRYSTAL

♦ Wear it.

♦ Carry it in your pocket.

♦ Meditate with it.

♦ Place it in a prominent place in your home or office.

♦ Use it as a center stone in a crystal grid.

You may find that you want to program your crystals for a short time, a long time, or maybe even for life! If you're working with a crystal to manifest something specific, you won't need the crystal to be programmed after your desire has manifested. Alternatively, if you are working with a crystal for personal protection, you might decide to keep it programmed for your entire life.

THE BEST CRYSTALS FOR PROGRAMMING

All crystals can be programmed, but crystals in the quartz family are the best option. Quartz is very stable, structured, and piezoelectric (meaning it generates electricity in response to pressure). Each of these traits makes quartz a master at storing energy. Did you know that quartz crystal is used for storing 5-D digital data? The process is called optical data storage and is performed with lasers. Crystals with memory stored in them in this way can save up to 360 terabytes' worth of data. That is a lot of data! It's pretty incredible what some crystals can do.

·•⋄ TIP ⋄•·

See the list of all crystals in the quartz family on page 28.

FOCUSING ON YOUR PURPOSE

Programming goes hand in hand with manifesting best practices. You must be able to hone in on your purpose for the crystal as much as you can.

YOU WANT YOUR ENERGY TO VIBRATE WITH WHAT IT IS THAT YOU DESIRE MOST.

Your energy will imprint your desires into your crystal. Take into consideration the size and shape of the crystal you're programming. Will you be wearing it or placing it somewhere in your home? Often, smaller crystals work better for programming so you can wear them or carry them.

There are a few situations where you might like to program a bigger crystal. Programming larger crystals can come in handy if you want to offer protection or healing to a larger area, like your home or office. In a situation like this, programming a spherical or organic-shaped stone that will radiate its energy in all directions is ideal.

·◦◊ TIP ◊◦·

Always cleanse crystals before programming them.

···◈ RAISING YOUR VIBRATION ◈···

When you program a crystal, your energy frequency must be in alignment with the kind of energy you want to program your crystal with. If you want to bring more love into your life, you'll need to raise your vibration to love. If you're feeling stressed, tired, and overwhelmed, your crystal will pick up on that instead.

What I mean when I say "raise your vibration" is the energy you're giving off. At the smallest level, we're all beings of energy. Our subtle body system, which includes our aura and chakras, controls the flow of energy in our bodies. Your aura, or field of energy that surrounds your physical body, is ever changing and sensitive. Your energy field can change from moment to moment, depending on your thoughts, mood, and physical health.

Because the subtle body is so sensitive, you have the power to raise your vibration anytime you want. There are a variety of ways to boost your energy frequency or vibration. You'll find that some of the techniques I suggest to raise your frequency are similar to the methods used to charge and cleanse your crystals.

HOW TO RAISE
YOUR VIBRATION

MEDITATE

EAT HIGH-
VIBRATIONAL
FOODS

DRINK
BLESSED
WATER

SPEND TIME
WITH HIGH-
VIBRATIONAL
PEOPLE

SELF-CARE

PRAY

SPEND
TIME IN
NATURE

DANCE

GET
CREATIVE

USE
SOUND
HEALING

I AM LOVE AND LIGHT

REPEAT A HIGH-
VIBRATIONAL
MANTRA
"I am love and light."

WORK WITH HIGH-
VIBRATIONAL
CRYSTALS
Selenite and kyanite

HOW TO PROGRAM A CRYSTAL

1. Ensure that you have 10 to 30 minutes of uninterrupted quiet time to program your crystal.

2. Cleanse your crystal (see chapter 3) and charge your crystal (see chapter 4). Do this before programming. Be sure to charge your crystal with an energy that matches your programming desire.

3. Raise your vibration to match that of your desire for the crystal you're programming. Try one of the techniques mentioned on pages 108 to 109 to raise your vibration.

4. Begin by focusing on your breath and centering yourself for 2 to 3 minutes.

5. Rub your hands together to activate the energy centers in your palms and warm them up.

6. Hold your crystal in your hands.

7. Close your eyes and visualize your goal. For example, if you want to manifest your dream job, imagine you're at your dream job.

8. Imagine how you'll feel when you're working at your dream job. Allow yourself to feel any emotions that come up.

9. Visualize your goal, and all of the emotions behind it, traveling from your third eye chakra (in between your eyebrows) into your crystal.

10. Hold your crystal and continue to meditate on your visualization, sending the information into it, for 5 to 30 minutes.

11. Your crystal is now programmed and will remain programmed for this purpose until you cleanse it.

If you program a crystal for a specific purpose, and that purpose is no longer needed, you'll want to cleanse the crystal to remove the programming. Programmed crystals will require more intense cleansing to remove all of the information. I suggest using two or three of the cleansing techniques in chapter 3 to cleanse your crystal. After you thoroughly cleanse it, you can use your crystal for anything you'd like or reprogram it for a new purpose.

CHAPTER 6

CRYSTAL
GRIDS

C rystal grids are a beautiful and powerful way to work with crystals. Placing crystals in specific grid patterns amplifies and unifies their energy. By repeating the perfect structures of crystals with more crystals and using the principles of sacred geometry, you create a vortex of energy that will intensify your goals and desires. The options for creating grids are endless and only limited by your creativity. You can design crystal grids for any purpose you need. I share several crystal grid "recipes" in this chapter to get you started.

I suggest using the crystal grids at the end of this chapter as a starting point. Each grid is open to your interpretation and can be modified to suit your needs. If I recommend a crystal that you don't have handy, check the correspondences for the crystal in the last chapter. Look for other crystals that have similar correspondences to replace any crystal listed. For example, if you're missing malachite from the Attracting Love crystal grid, it could be replaced with moss agate, rhodochrosite, or fuchsite because they all have similar correspondences.

YOU ARE WORTHY OF ALL
THAT YOU DESIRE.

SACRED GEOMETRY AND CRYSTAL GRIDS

Sacred geometry symbols are divinely inspired patterns that are found in nature, our DNA, architecture, artwork, and sacred texts. Sacred geometry patterns were recognized as divine and powerful symbols very early on in humanity. The symbols themselves are said to be a blueprint of creation and hold the keys to the Universe. Humans have assigned special meaning to sacred geometry since the beginning of time.

Sacred geometry lends itself to working with crystals because, like crystals, it is created from perfect repeating patterns. Specific sacred geometry symbols can be used in grids to add another layer of intention and further amplify your goals. Using these symbols for your crystal grid will also make it easier to create your grid in a balanced way.

> ## ·•◊ TIP ◊•·
> You can find sacred geometry symbols to print by doing a quick internet search, or at my blog (see the link on page 158). Many artists create cloth or wood mats with sacred geometry on them, perfect for crystal gridding.

SACRED GEOMETRY SYMBOLS

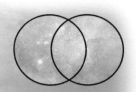

CIRCLE
Oneness, Connection
to Source Energy

TRIANGLE
Strength,
Trinities

VESICA PISCIS
Femininity, New
Beginnings

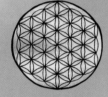

SEED OF LIFE
Potential, Growth

FLOWER OF LIFE
Community, Connection

SRI YANTRA
Balance, Meditation

METATRON'S CUBE
Energy, Protection

SELECTING THE RIGHT CRYSTALS FOR YOUR GRID

You will need crystals for three different purposes for your grid: a center stone, secondary stones, and an activation stone. The activation stone is optional, but you need to have a center stone and at least three secondary stones.

- ♦ **Center Stone**: Usually, a larger stone to be placed at the center of your grid, used to radiate your desires outward.

- ♦ **Secondary Stones**: Smaller stones placed evenly around the center stone, used to amplify your intention and connect the energy of the crystals on your grid.

- ♦ **Activation Stone (optional)**: Pointed crystal used to activate your grid.

> ## ·◦◁ TIP ▷◦·
>
> **You don't need fifty different crystals to make a crystal grid. One center stone that's in alignment with your goal and a handful of quartz is enough to make a powerful crystal grid.**

◁◡ CRYSTAL SHAPE PROPERTIES ◡▷

Crystals form into unique shapes as they grow, but many are cut and polished into a variety of other shapes. The shapes of the crystals that you select for your grid will affect the energy of your grid. There are specific crystal shapes that will amplify the energy of your grid in specific ways. Even if you don't have the shape of a crystal you think will work best, your crystal grid will still work. Don't let not having a specific crystal shape stop you from creating a grid. This chart explains how each crystal shape disperses energy, and whether it works better as a center stone or a secondary stone.

TUMBLED
- ◆ Secondary stone
- ◆ Radiates energy in a variety of directions, depending on its shape

SPHERE OR EGG
- ◆ Center stone
- ◆ Radiates energy equally in all directions

TOWER OR OBELISK
- ◆ Center stone or activation stone
- ◆ Radiates energy upward

PYRAMID
- ◆ Center stone
- ◆ Concentrates energy and radiates it upward

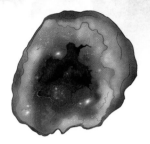

CLUSTER OR GEODE

♦ Center stone

♦ Sends energy in the directions of its points

TERMINATED AND DOUBLE TERMINATED

♦ Secondary stone or activation stone

♦ Sends energy in the direction of its point(s)

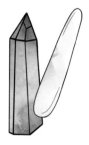

ROUGH

♦ Center stone or secondary stone

♦ Similar to tumbled stone but energy will be less smooth and more jagged

WAND

♦ Activation stone

♦ Sends energy in the direction of its point

WHEN TO USE YOUR CRYSTAL GRID

The timing of when you set up and take down your grid can have an energetic impact on your grid and results. The weekdays and moon phases each have corresponding energies assigned to them. I share the energy associated with each weekday and moon phase in the coming pages. I've simplified the moon phases here in this chapter to simply waxing and waning energy because you will likely want to leave your crystal grid up for a minimum of half a lunar cycle. If you want to revisit the energy associated with each lunar phase, you can check it out on page 99.

I suggest setting up your crystal grid when the moon phase and day of the week are in energetic alignment with the intention of your grid. Think of this as adding an additional layer of intention to your grid. For example, if you're creating a crystal grid for attracting love, the best moon phase that creates your grid is during any waxing moon phase, and the best day is Friday. The waxing moon phase corresponds to growth and expansion, and Friday is associated with love. By setting up your grid at this time you're signaling to the Universe that you want more love in your life.

There are a couple of options for taking down your crystal grid. I like to leave my crystal grids up for a full lunar cycle. So, if I placed my crystal grid on a new moon, I would wait until the following new moon to take it down. If you create a crystal grid for releasing a habit, you might decide to leave your grid up for the waning moon phase and take it down at the dark moon. Alternatively, if you create a crystal grid to manifest something in your life and what you desire manifests, you may decide to take down your grid when your desire is manifested. As always, when working with crystal energy, trust your intuition.

I share a suggested moon phase and day of the week for each of the crystal grid "recipes" on pages 126 to 135. In general, the waxing moon phase is ideal for anything related to growth, and the waning moon phase is related to anything pertaining to releasing.

SUGGESTED DAY OF THE WEEK FOR CRYSTAL GRIDS

- **Monday**: Intuition
- **Tuesday**: Strength
- **Wednesday**: Expression
- **Thursday**: Abundance
- **Friday**: Love
- **Saturday**: Protection
- **Sunday**: Growth

SUGGESTED MOON PHASE
FOR CRYSTAL GRID

WAXING MOON PHASE

The waxing moon phase occurs from the new moon to the height of the full moon.

- Abundance
- Accomplishing goals
- Energy
- Growth
- Love
- Manifesting
- New beginnings
- Success

WANING MOON PHASE

The waning moon phase occurs right after the full moon to the dark moon phase.

- Acceptance
- Cleansing
- Cord-cutting
- Letting go
- Overcoming fear
- Protection
- Releasing stress and anxiety
- Rest

CREATING YOUR CRYSTAL GRID

Follow these steps to create any of the grids suggested in this chapter or to create a crystal grid of your own. If you're working with a crystal grid I share in this chapter, I provide suggestions for many of these steps.

1. SET AN INTENTION.

Your intention for your grid is your starting place and will lay the foundation for everything else you choose for your grid. Get quiet and breathe for a few minutes to gain complete clarity about what it is you want.

·◦ TIP ◦·

Write down your intention for your crystal grid on a small piece of paper, and place the piece of paper under the center stone of your grid.

---

2. SELECT YOUR GRID FORMAT.

Select a sacred geometry symbol for the outline of your grid. Pick something that matches your intention. For example, if you're creating a crystal grid for abundance, the Seed of Life symbol is a great option.

3. SELECT YOUR CRYSTALS.

Now, the fun part! Select your crystals. If you're following one of my grid suggestions in this chapter, collect the suggested stones. If you're creating your own grid, see chapter 7 for crystal suggestions. Your center stone should be the biggest crystal and be a shape that is conducive to sending your intention outward. Your secondary stones should be smaller than your center stone and a form that is conducive to sharing their energy among the other crystals on the grid.

4. CLEANSE.

Cleanse your crystals, yourself, and the room in which you're creating your grid. You don't want any lingering bad vibes playing a role in your manifesting!

> ### TIP
> Any crystal cleansing technique you use can also be used on yourself and your environment.

5. CHARGE YOUR CRYSTALS.

Charge all of your crystals with an energy that matches your intention.

> ### TIP
> Consider programming your center stone to add an extra boost of manifesting energy to your grid (see chapter 5).

◄〜 6. PLACE YOUR CRYSTALS. 〜►

Place your center stone first. Next, carefully place your secondary stones around the center stone in a balanced pattern. As you place each stone, visualize your intent for the grid coming true.

◄〜 7. ACTIVATE YOUR GRID. 〜►

Think of activating your grid as turning it on. You've set everything up; now it's showtime! There's more than one way to activate your grid. The simplest method is to close your eyes and imagine the energy of all your crystals connecting. This method is the easiest and fastest way to activate your crystal grid. Activating your grid helps all the crystals on the grid work together to accomplish your goal.

A second technique is where your activation point crystal comes in. To use your activation crystal to activate your grid, hold it in your hand like a wand. Use your giving hand for this step (this will likely be your dominant hand). Hovering above each crystal, connect all of them, like a "dot-to-dot" picture. Activating your grid this way takes longer but feels so nice. Try for yourself to see what I mean.

◄〜 8. BE PRESENT WITH YOUR GRID DAILY. 〜►

Don't just set it and forget it! For your crystal grid to work, you'll want to make contact with it every day. Connecting with your grid daily will allow you to visualize your desires and goals regularly.

⊰⌣ 9. DISASSEMBLE YOUR GRID. ⌣⊱

You can leave your grid up for as long as you like. I suggest keeping it up for a minimum of one lunar cycle, or about a month. You'll want to cleanse all of the crystals on your grid before using them again.

⋯◈ CRYSTAL GRIDS BY NEED ◈⋯

On the following pages, I share a variety of crystal grids by need. Use the crystal grids in the following pages as is, or as reference points and creative jumping-off points. Remember, if there's a crystal listed in one of these grids that you don't have, that's okay. See chapter 7 for other crystal suggestions.

> ### ⋅◦◊ TIP ◊◦⋅
>
> **Use clear quartz as a stand-in for any crystal you don't have.**

ATTRACTING LOVE

Use this crystal grid to attract romantic love, compassion, or self-love into your life.

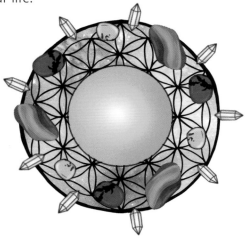

·•◊ SACRED GEOMETRY ◊•·
Flower of Life or Vesica Pisces

·•◊ MANTRA ◊•·
"I am love and welcome love into my life."

·•◊ CENTER STONE ◊•·
Rose quartz sphere

·•◊ SECONDARY STONES ◊•·
Quartz, rhodonite, malachite, prehnite

·•◊ SUGGESTED MOON PHASE ◊•·
Waxing phase

·•◊ SUGGESTED DAY ◊•·
Friday

⊰⌣ ATTRACTING WEALTH ⌣⊱

Use this crystal grid to attract more financial security into your life.

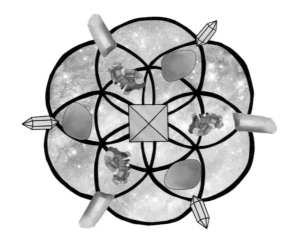

·•◊ SACRED GEOMETRY ◊•·
Seed of Life

·•◊ MANTRA ◊•·
"Money flows to me with ease."

·•◊ CENTER STONE ◊•·
Quartz tower

·•◊ SECONDARY STONES ◊•·
Citrine, green aventurine, pyrite, quartz

·•◊ SUGGESTED MOON PHASE ◊•·
Waxing phase

·•◊ SUGGESTED DAY ◊•·
Sunday

◄◡ **ATTAINING YOUR GOALS** ◡►

Use this crystal grid to help you meet your goals.

·●◊ SACRED GEOMETRY ◊●·
Triangle

·●◊ MANTRA ◊●·
"I have everything I need to accomplish my goals."

·●◊ CENTER STONE ◊●·
Tiger's eye tower

·●◊ SECONDARY STONES ◊●·
Fluorite, smoky quartz, yellow jasper, red jasper

·●◊ SUGGESTED MOON PHASE ◊●·
Waxing phase

·●◊ SUGGESTED DAY ◊●·
Tuesday

HEALTHY BODY

Use this crystal grid to bring a sense of health and vitality to your being.

·•◊ SACRED GEOMETRY ◊•·
Metatron's Cube or Sri Yantra

·•◊ MANTRA ◊•·
"I trust my body's ability to heal itself."

·•◊ CENTER STONE ◊•·
Quartz sphere

·•◊ SECONDARY STONES ◊•·
Bloodstone, carnelian, amethyst, lapis lazuli, quartz

·•◊ SUGGESTED MOON PHASE ◊•·
Dark moon

·•◊ SUGGESTED DAY ◊•·
Saturday

PEACEFUL SPACE

Use this crystal grid to alleviate stress and bring a sense of peace to your environment.

SACRED GEOMETRY
Circle

MANTRA
"I invite peace into this space."

CENTER STONE
Tumbled or raw blue lace agate

SECONDARY STONES
Amethyst, aquamarine, rose quartz, lepidolite

SUGGESTED MOON PHASE
Full, new, or dark moon

SUGGESTED DAY
Saturday

Use this crystal grid to release anything that's no longer serving you.

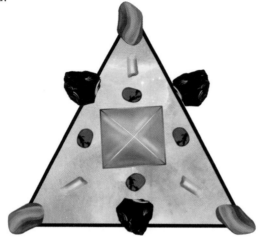

·•◁ SACRED GEOMETRY ◁•·
Triangle

·•◁ MANTRA ◁•·
"I release everything that no longer serves me."

·•◁ CENTER STONE ◁•·
Smoky quartz tower

·•◁ SECONDARY STONES ◁•·
Obsidian, malachite, rhodonite, citrine

·•◁ SUGGESTED MOON PHASE ◁•·
Waning phase or dark moon

·•◁ SUGGESTED DAY ◁•·
Saturday

◄〜 PROTECTION 〜►

Use this crystal grid to offer yourself and your space energetic protection.

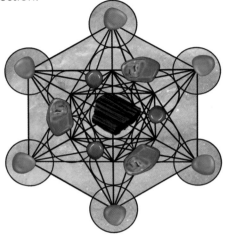

·•◊ SACRED GEOMETRY ◊•·
Metatron's Cube

·•◊ MANTRA ◊•·
"My energy is safe and protected."

·•◊ CENTER STONE ◊•·
Raw or tumbled black tourmaline

·•◊ SECONDARY STONES ◊•·
Hematite, amethyst, labradorite

·•◊ SUGGESTED MOON PHASE ◊•·
Dark moon, full moon, or waning phase

·•◊ SUGGESTED DAY ◊•·
Saturday

INTUITION ENHANCEMENT

Use this crystal grid to connect with your psychic gifts.

·•◊ SACRED GEOMETRY ◊•·
Sri Yantra, Circle, or Seed of Life

·•◊ MANTRA ◊•·
"I am open to psychic information."

·•◊ CENTER STONE ◊•·
Amethyst sphere

·•◊ SECONDARY STONES ◊•·
Celestite, moonstone, apophyllite, labradorite

·•◊ SUGGESTED MOON PHASE ◊•·
Full moon

·•◊ SUGGESTED DAY ◊•·
Monday

⊲〰 **COMMUNICATION AMPLIFICATION** 〰⊳

Use this crystal grid to help you communicate more effectively.

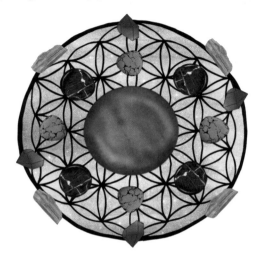

·●◊ SACRED GEOMETRY ◁●·
Flower of Life or Vesica Piscis

·●◊ MANTRA ◁●·
"I express myself with ease."

·●◊ CENTER STONE ◁●·
Chrysocolla sphere

·●◊ SECONDARY STONES ◁●·
Kyanite, sodalite, amethyst, turquoise

·●◊ SUGGESTED MOON PHASE ◁●·
Waxing phase or full moon

·●◊ SUGGESTED DAY ◁●·
Wednesday

CREATIVITY

Use this crystal grid to bring a flow of creativity into your life or a specific project.

·•◊ SACRED GEOMETRY ◊•·
Flower of Life or Vesica Piscis

·•◊ MANTRA ◊•·
"Creativity flows through me."

·•◊ CENTER STONE ◊•·
Carnelian sphere or tumbled stone

·•◊ SECONDARY STONES ◊•·
Rainbow moonstone, larimar, kunzite, orange calcite

·•◊ SUGGESTED MOON PHASE ◊•·
Waxing phase or full moon

·•◊ SUGGESTED DAY ◊•·
Wednesday

CHAPTER 7

CRYSTAL GUIDE

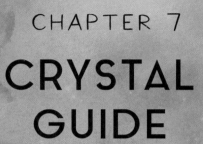

This illustrated crystal guide can serve as a quick reference for working with the energy of crystals. I offer two descriptive words for each stone and their corresponding zodiac sign, moon phase, and chakra. The correspondences are a fast way to understand the energy of each crystal on a deeper level.

Don't let a specific correspondence stop you from working with a crystal. If a stone you feel called to corresponds to Aquarius, for example, and you're a Leo, you can still work with that crystal. The correspondence of Aquarius means that the crystal carries energy well suited for Aquarians. You might need the same healing energy.

MAY YOUR CRYSTAL JOURNEY SERVE AS A POWERFUL TOOL FOR MANIFESTING THE ENERGY YOU'RE TRYING TO BRING INTO YOUR LIFE.

·◦◊ TIP ◊◦·

Learn more about the energy of each moon phase on page 99.

WHAT ARE CORRESPONDENCES?

Correspondences reveal symbols and tools that carry similar energies. Understanding correspondences can greatly enhance your spiritual practice and bring more meaning to working with crystals. They're also a quick way to comprehend the energy of a particular item.

···◆ CORRESPONDENCE KEY ◆···

ZODIAC	MOON PHASE	CHAKRA
Aquarius	New Moon	Earth Star Chakra
Pisces	Waxing Crescent	Root Chakra
Aries	First Quarter	Sacral Chakra
Taurus	Waxing Gibbous	Solar Plexus Chakra
Gemini	Full Moon	Heart Chakra
Cancer	Waning Gibbous	Throat Chakra
Leo	Last Quarter	Third Eye Chakra
Virgo	Waning Crescent	Crown Chakra
Libra	Dark Moon	Soul Star Chakra
Scorpio	All Moon Phases	All Chakras
Sagittarius		
Capricorn		
All Zodiacs		

···✦ CRYSTALS ✦···

AMAZONITE
Honesty & Heart Healing

AMBER
Stability & Intellect

    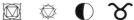

AMETHYST
Spirituality & Guarding

AMETRINE
Clarity & Releasing Blocks

AMMOLITE
Energy & Harmony

     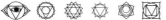

ANGELITE
Angelic Connection & Awareness

APOPHYLLITE
Akashic Records & Reiki Healing

AQUAMARINE
Courage & Calming

ARAGONITE
Centering & Earth Awareness

AZURITE
Intuition & New Perspectives

BERTRANDITE
(TIFFANY STONE)
Freedom & Releasing

BLACK KYANITE
Psychic Protection & Grounding

BLACK TOURMALINE
Negativity Shield & Positivity

BLOODSTONE
Purifying & Mental Clarity

BLUE APATITE
Motivation & Expression

BLUE CHALCEDONY
Nurturing & Peace

BLUE KYANITE
Connection & Truth

BLUE LACE AGATE
Peace & Support

BLUE TOPAZ
Manifesting & Aspirations

CARNELIAN
Vitality & Ambition

CELESTITE
Enlightenment & Bliss

CHAROITE
Overcoming & Breaking Patterns

CHRYSOCOLLA
Communication & Empowerment

CHRYSOPRASE
Happiness & Letting Go

CINNABAR
Virtue & Wealth

CITRINE
Joy & Abundance

CLEAR QUARTZ
Ultimate Healer & Balancer

DALMATIAN JASPER
Determination & Harmonizing

DANBURITE
Cutting Cords & Clearing

DUMORTIERITE
Confidence & Calming

EMERALD
Wisdom & Achievement

FLUORITE
Clarity & Anxiety Reduction

FUCHSITE
Renewal & Growth

GARNET
Energizing & Strengthening

GRAPE AGATE
Support & Trust

GREEN AVENTURINE
Opportunity & Expansion

GREEN CALCITE
Comfort & Healing

GREEN JASPER
Earth Energy & Balance

GREY MOONSTONE
Potential & Lunar Wisdom

HALITE
Cleansing & Purifying

HEMATITE
Shielding & Protective

HERKIMER DIAMOND
Unity & Spiritual Growth

HOWLITE
Calming & Sleep Aid

IOLITE
Awareness & Journey Work

JADEITE
Blessings & Protection

KAMMERERITE
**Spiritual Development &
Interconnectedness**

KUNZITE
Unconditional Love & Healing

LABRADORITE
Psychic Protection & Aura Repair

LAPIS LAZULI
Wisdom & Power

LARIMAR
Tranquility & Serenity

LARVIKITE
Psychic Work & Grounding

LEPIDOLITE
Transformation & Letting Go

MAGNESITE
Soothe & Harmonize

MALACHITE
Amplification & Transformation

MANGANO CALCITE
Love & Patience

MOLDAVITE
Cosmic Connection & Transcendence

MOOKAITE
Stability & Practicality

MORGANITE
Gentleness & Fairness

MOSS AGATE
New Beginnings & Growth

OBSIDIAN
Honesty & Blockages

ONYX
Integration & Confidence

OPAL
Creativity & Amplification

OPTICAL CALCITE
Amplifying & Clarifying

ORANGE CALCITE
Energy & Emotional Support

PERIDOT
Purifying & Cleansing

PIETERSITE
Highly Spiritual & Psychic Work

PREHNITE

Deep Healing & Precognition

PYRITE

Opportunity & Assertiveness

RAINBOW MOONSTONE

Wisdom & Flow

RED JASPER

Courage & Grounding

RHODOCHROSITE

**Healthy Relationships &
Compassion**

RHODONITE

**Emotional Balancer &
Heart Healing**

ROSE QUARTZ
Self-Love & Unconditional Love

RUBY
Sensuality & Passion

RUTILATED QUARTZ
Illumination & Manifesting

SAPPHIRE
Alignment & Wisdom

SCOLECITE
Cooperation & Connection

SELENITE
Light Bearer & Cleansing

SERPENTINE

Kundalini Energy & Healing

SHATTUCKITE

Perception & Communication

SHIVA LINGAM

Vitality & Egolessness

SHUNGITE

Shielding & Healing

SMOKY QUARTZ

Tension Reliever & Grounding

SNOWFLAKE OBSIDIAN

Shadow Work & Balance

SODALITE

Expression & Communication

SPIRIT QUARTZ

Spiritual Connection & Truth

SUGILITE

Soul Purpose & Empath Protection

SUNSTONE

Joy & Independence

SUPER 7
(MELODY'S STONE)

Harmony & Transcendence

TANZANITE

Intuition & Psychic Abilities

TIGER'S EYE
Good Fortune & Protection

 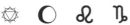

TURQUOISE
Travel Protection & Empowerment

UNAKITE
Regeneration & Balance

WATERMELON TOURMALINE
Emotional Stability & Confidence

WULFENITE
Integration & Karmic Balance

YELLOW JASPER
Self-Confidence & Intellect

MESSAGE FROM THE AUTHOR

Crystals are here to help us. By working with crystal energy, you're choosing to be in alignment with your true nature. Crystals have been here long before we have. They retain all of the wisdom of Mother Earth within them. They are powerful healers that should be held with the utmost respect.

My hope is that through this book you learn to feel the energy of crystals and allow them to raise your vibration. Your efforts to raise your vibration will raise the vibration of the people closest to you, which will in turn continue the forward motion of the evolution of the human spirit.

Let your goals and desires be amplified by the power of crystals so that you can bring your truest self forward.

Love 🤍 Light

Cassie

THANK YOU

Endless gratitude to those who made this book series possible!
Thank you to all of the sweet souls at Quarto Publishing,
especially to my editor, Keyla. Thank you to my designer,
Sydney, who's been a creative force for Zenned Out since its
inception many years ago. Sincere gratitude to my infinitely
patient husband who, unwaveringly and lovingly, supports
every new journey I embark on. Eternal gratitude to my guides
on the other side, including my sweet grandmother and father.
Special thanks to Phyllicia Bonanno for being my singing bowl
Goddess on page 109.

Thank you to every single one of my fans, followers, and
supporters. I see you, and I love you. You light me up every
day and give me the energy to continue sharing my gifts.

Love ♥ Light

Cassie

⋯•◈ ABOUT THE AUTHOR ◈•⋯

Cassie Uhl is an artist, author, empath, and the lead Goddess of her business Zenned Out. She created Zenned Out with the mission to build a brand that normalizes spirituality. It is her goal to offer accessible information to enable you to understand a variety of spiritual practices and put them into action. She provides an abundance of free information and printable tools on her blog at ZennedOut.com/Blog.

Cassie has been meditating and working with her energy since her teenage years. In 2012, she expanded her spiritual practice by receiving her 200 Hour Yoga Teacher Training License. She continues to explore and grow her spiritual knowledge and share ways for you to dive deeper into yours.

Through Zenned Out, Cassie has self-published her best-selling *Goddess Discovery Books* and oracle card deck, *The Ritual Deck*. Her work and writing have been featured at Astrology.com, *Goddess Provisions*, *Women's Day Magazine*, and *The Cosmic Calling Podcast*. Learn more about Cassie and her other products at ZennedOut.com.

·❖ REFERENCES ❖·

Ahlquist, Diane. *Moon Spells: How to Use the Phases of the Moon to Get What You Want.* Avon, MA: Adams Media, 2002.

"Crystal Structure and Crystal Systems." Geology In. www.geologyin.com/2014/11/crystal-structure-and-crystal-system.html.

Fogg, Kiera. *Crystal Gridwork: The Power of Crystals and Sacred Geometry to Heal, Protect, and Inspire.* Beverly, MA: Quarto Publishing, 2018.

Gienger, Michael. *Purifying Crystals: How to Clear, Charge, and Purify Your Healing Crystals.* Rochester, VT: Earthdancer Books, 2008.

Hall, Judy. *The Crystal Bible: A Definitive Guide to Crystals.* Blue Ash, OH: Walking Stick Press, 2003.

Hall, Judy. *Crystal Healing.* New York: Hachette Book Group, 2005.

Hall, Judy. "How Crystals Work: The Science of Crystal Healing." You Can Heal Your Life. 2016. www.healyourlife.com/how-crystals-work-the-science-of-crystal-healing.

Kynes, Sandra. *Llewellyn's Complete Book of Correspondences: A Comprehensive & Cross-Referenced Resource for Pagans & Wiccans.* Woodbury, MN: Llewellyn Publications, 2013.

Lazzerini, Ethan. *Crystal Grids Power: Harness the Power of Crystals & Sacred Geometry for Manifesting Abundance, Healing & Protection.* Scotts Valley, CA: CreateSpace, 2017.

Leavy, Ashley. *Crystals for Energy Healing: A Practical Sourcebook of 100 Crystals.* Beverly, MA: Quarto Publishing, 2017.

Mercier, Patricia. *The Chakra Bible: The Definitive Guide to Working with Chakras.* New York: Sterling Publishing Co., 2007.

Moon, Hibiscus. "Which Crystal Is the Most Powerful?" Hibiscus Moon. https://hibiscusmooncrystalacademy.com/which-crystal-is-the-most-powerful.

Uhl, Cassie. *The Goddess Discovery Book: Magick & Nature.* Tempe, AZ: Zenned Out, 2019.